DiaBeTes snacks, Treats & easy eats

130 Recipes You'll Make Again and Again

Barbara Grunes
with **Linda R. Yoakam**, R.D. M.S.

S
SURREY
BOOKS

First edition: 5

This book is manufactured in the United States of America

Library of Congress Cataloging-in-Publication Data:

Grunes, Barbara.
   Diabetes snacks, treats & easy eats : 150 recipes you'll make again and again /
by Barbara Grunes, with Linda R. Yoakam.
   p. cm.
   ISBN 1-57284-060-9
   1. Diabetes—Diet therapy—Recipes. I. Title: Diabetes snacks, treats, and easy eats.
II. Yoakam, Linda R. III. Title.
   RC662.G725 2004
   641.5'6314—dc22

                                                2003021978

Surrey Books is an imprint of Agate Publishing, Inc.
Editorial services: Bookcrafters, Inc., Chicago
Art direction, book design, and production: Joan Sommers Design, Chicago
Nutritional analyses: Linda R. Yoakam, R.D., M.S.

Surrey and Agate books can be purchased in bulk at discounted prices.
For more information, go to agatepublishing.com.

ACKNOWLEDGMENTS

Thanks and appreciation go to my special friend Virginia Van Vynckt for her advice and editing; Chris Young for his endless help with the computer; and Chris's beautiful wife, Dorothy, for her encouragement. Additional thanks go to Linda Yoakam, M.S., R.D., L.D., for nutritional analyses; Dr. Debra Edidin, M.D., for medical guidance; and Jenny Edidin for recipe testing. Also deserving thanks are editors Gene DeRoin and Karen Straus, editorial assistant Anna Layton, and publisher Susan Schwartz.

And a very special thanks to my husband, Jerry, who makes all things possible for me.

CONTENTS

FOREWORD

When my friend and neighbor asked me to write a Foreword to her new cookbook, *Diabetes Snacks, Treats & Easy Eats*, we had a lengthy discussion about the book's point of view. After all, there are no longer any "taboo" foods for people with diabetes.

As a nation, however, we are fat and our children are, too. American children have a 30 percent chance of becoming obese adults. We have learned that being overweight dramatically increases the chances of developing diabetes and greatly increases the health risks and complications for a person with diabetes. And like overweight adults, our children are developing diabetes in numbers that are truly frightening. Children are no longer the victims of just Type 1, or juvenile, diabetes; they are now falling prey to Type 2, a preventable disease that used to strike primarily older adults.

Today, adults and children with diabetes are working with their doctor, registered dietitian, or certified diabetes educator to develop individualized eating plans. They are learning about portion control, how to count carbohydrates or exchanges, and, for those who take insulin, how to adjust their insulin doses accordingly.

We need to do something now to stop this epidemic, and we need to start with our children. As parents, healthcare providers, and caretakers, we should focus on how to encourage the consumption of good, wholesome foods, not on how to make junk food less junky.

This book is Barbara's contribution toward that end. She provides recipes for nutritious foods that are easy to prepare and delicious to eat. She also makes it do-able for the time-challenged home cook by limiting recipes to as few ingredients as possible. Complete nutritional information, including exchanges, is provided for each recipe.

Until the final research work is in, and until you have a chance to develop—with a healthcare provider—an individualized eating plan for yourself or your child, there are several ways to improve your current health and safeguard your future health: Practice portion control; eat a variety of foods, especially whole grains and colorful vegetables and fruits; reach and/or maintain a suitable weight; and make exercise a daily part of your life.

—Debra Edidin, M. D.
Pediatric Endocrinologist
Northwestern University Medical School

INTRODUCTION

"Contrary to popular myth, there is no 'diabetes diet.'" So states the Mayo Clinic newsletter. In fact, medical and nutritional professionals have transformed the diabetes diets of yesteryear into contemporary meal planning that includes just about any foods you like as long as nutrition, balance, and portion control are given careful attention.

No longer are foods labeled as "good," "bad," or "forbidden." No longer does a diagnosis of diabetes mean a life sentence of bland, boring, and unappetizing meals.

Diabetes Snacks, Treats & Easy Eats offers a wide range of recipes from appetizers to desserts and accompanies each with the nutritional information you need to stay within your meal-planning goals.

Even though people with diabetes do not have to give up favorite dishes and snacks they like, including sugar used sparingly and the occasional sweet, it is important to plan meals carefully, both for nutritional quality and quantity. It is even more important for those with diabetes than for the general population to choose foods that are low in fat, moderate in carbohydrates, low in salt, high in fiber, and rich in vitamins and minerals because people with diabetes are at higher risk for heart disease and a host of other health concerns as a result of their condition. Diabetes medications also work better when used in conjunction with a healthy diet and regular exercise.

Finding the calorie level that is right for your body's needs, your age, and your activity level is, of course, essential. And even though you can eat moderate portions of just about anything, excess body weight is a serious threat to controlling diabetes and preventing heart disease and other complications that might arise from it.

BALANCING WHAT YOU EAT

For people with diabetes, controlling carbohydrate intake can be of major importance since carbohydrates raise glucose levels faster and more dramatically than other foods. Carbohydrates are found in foods with natural or added sugar such as breads, pasta, rice, crackers, cereals, potatoes, fresh fruits and juices, milk, table sugar, jams, and jellies. Other foods contain carbohydrates in combination with proteins and fats; some examples are cakes, ice cream, doughnuts, pizza, potato chips, and soups.

Table sugar used to be a "forbidden" food. It is now allowed in small amounts when needed for taste or texture, as long as it is counted with the total carbohydrate intake. Researchers have found that sugar does not raise blood glucose levels more rapidly than other foods containing carbohydrates. What is important is the total amount of carbohydrates eaten, not their source.

But beware: sweets and other foods high in sugar may also be high in fat and low in fiber and other nutrients. A diet high in fiber can help people with diabetes lower their blood sugar and insulin levels by as much as 10 percent. Fiber helps slow the rate at which your body digests and absorbs carbohydrates in food. So a choice between an apple and a doughnut is still an easy one to make.

A healthy and nutritious meal plan will include a variety of foods found in the U.S. Department of Agriculture Food Guide Pyramid and the Diabetes Food Pyramid. These include bread or other starches, preferably made from whole grains; fruit, nonfat milk, vegetables, low-fat meats, fish, and poultry; and the right kinds of fats, such as walnuts and olive and canola oils, used sparingly.

Although specific nutrition goals that reflect blood glucose targets and other medical aims should be discussed with your doctor, registered dietitian, or certified diabetes educator, the following guidelines for daily allowances of carbohydrate, protein, and fat can form the basis of a balanced meal plan.

Calories per day	50% calories Carbohydrates	20% calories Protein	30% calories Fat
1500	188 gm	75 gm	50 gm
1800	225 gm	90 gm	60 gm
2000	250 gm	100 gm	66 gm
2200	275 gm	110 gm	73 gm

Knowing your individual carbohydrate, protein, and fat needs will help you choose recipes that meet these goals, and you can continue to eat most of your favorite foods. If you look at the nutritional information provided with every recipe in *Diabetes Snacks, Treats & Easy Eats*, you will be surprised at what a wide variety of foods you can enjoy while staying within your individualized eating plan goals.

Note, too, that consistency is very important. To keep blood sugar at optimum levels, try to eat the same quantity of food and the same proportions of carbohydrate, protein, and fat each day and at the same time of day. You may need to make adjustments in your eating plan to accommodate for sick days or for increased or reduced activity.

THE EXCHANGE SYSTEM VS. COUNTING CARBS

A variety of meal-planning strategies can be used to control your diabetes. Keep in mind that there is no single meal plan that is appropriate for everyone. Individualizing your meal plan is the key to successful control of blood glucose levels. Also remember that, as discussed by the American Diabetes Association and the American Dietetic Association, meal planning for diabetes is really little more than establishing a healthy way of eating. People with diabetes today eat the same foods as people without diabetes.

Two popular meal-planning strategies are in wide use among people with diabetes. One is the exchange system, in which foods are divided into six basic food groups according to the nutrients they contain. Foods in the same group with similar nutrients can be exchanged, or substituted, for one another to meet the daily-allowed quantity of that particular food group. A registered dietitian or certified diabetes educator can best assist people in deciding how many exchanges, or servings, of which foods should be allowed at each meal.

However, until meeting with a registered dietitian or certified diabetes educator, the following meal plan can serve as a guide. To use the exchange list method, simply compare the number of exchanges recommended in the chart below with the number shown in the nutritional data for each recipe.

Breakfast	A.M. Snack	Lunch	P.M. Snack	Dinner	Bedtime
2 bread	1 bread	3 meat	1 fruit	3 bread	2 bread
1 fruit		2 bread		3 meat	1 meat
1 milk		1 fruit		2 veg.	
1 meat		1 veg.		1 fat	
1 fat		1 milk			
		1 fat			

Another method of meal planning for people with diabetes is to count the number of carbohydrate grams eaten. This number is given for each recipe in the book to help a person using this method stay within daily prescribed limits and yet enjoy a wide variety of foods.

Of course, for a balanced diet one needs more than just carbohydrates, so we have included suggested quantities of other nutrients in this sample meal plan.

Breakfast	A.M. Snack	Lunch	P.M. Snack	Dinner	Bedtime
60 gm carb.	15 gm carb.	45 gm carb.	15 gm carb.	55 gm carb.	15 gm carb.
1 oz. meat		2 oz. meat		3 oz. meat	
1 tsp. fat		½ cup veg.		1 cup veg.	
		1 tsp. fat		1 tsp. fat	

NUTRITIONAL INFORMATION

Today, cooking healthy meals is a snap thanks to a variety of new food products made with less fat, sodium, and sugar. Reduced-fat cheeses, low-sodium broth and canned beans, and sugar-free ice cream and instant pudding mixes are readily available. Lettuces and spinach are pre-washed and packaged for convenience; carrots and cabbage are shredded and packaged. In addition, flavorful low-sodium spice mixes abound, and there are a variety of sugar substitutes, from spoonable forms for baking to convenient single-serve packets, for those wishing to reduce their total calorie and carbohydrate intake.

The recipes in *Diabetes Snacks, Treats & Easy Eats* were created using the highest quality ingredients available and were designed to use some convenience products to save time. Eating sensibly should not have to mean extra time in the kitchen, so recipes have been kept simple and easy.

Low-fat meats such as skinless chicken breasts, beef eye of round, and pork tenderloin were selected instead of higher-fat cuts. Many nutritious fat-free and reduced-fat dairy products are called for such as fat-free milk, fat-free half-and-half, reduced-fat cheeses, and low-fat sour cream. Egg whites and liquid egg substitute were often chosen in place of their higher-cholesterol equivalents. Fat-free, reduced-sodium broths were mainly used. Vegetable cooking spray usually replaces higher-fat liquid oils for cooking. A variety of herbs, spices, and seasonings enhance flavors while keeping sodium content down.

Recipes throughout the book reflect the nutritional standards and follow the guidelines recommended by the United States

Department of Agriculture for the general population as well as for people with diabetes:

- Eat a variety of foods
- Choose a diet with plenty of grain products, vegetables, and fruit
- Choose a diet low in fat, saturated fat, and cholesterol
- Choose a diet moderate in sugars
- Choose a diet moderate in salt and sodium
- If you drink alcoholic beverages, do so in moderation

In addition to specific nutritional information and exchanges for each recipe, we have identified recipes that are especially low in carbohydrate, fat, and sodium.

⏱ **Low-carbohydrate recipe**
Contains 15 grams or less of carbohydrate (1 exchange) per serving

🐷 **Low-fat recipe**
Contains 3 grams or less of fat per serving

◇ **Low-sodium recipe**
Contains 140 mg or less of sodium per serving

Nutritional analyses and exchanges provided with each recipe were calculated by an independent nutrition consulting firm using an industry-standard nutritional software program. Nutritional information is meant to be used as a guideline only. Figures are based on laboratory values of ingredients, so results may vary slightly depending on the brand of ingredient used and the method of preparation. Other factors that can affect the accuracy of nutritional data include variability in sizes, weights, and measures of fruits, vegetables, and other foods. There is also a possible 20 percent error factor in the nutritional labeling of prepared foods.

Exchange values are averages. If the carbohydrate content of a day's intake is estimated using the exchanges shown, there may be a significant difference between the estimate and the actual values consumed.

Ingredients noted as "optional," "to taste," or "as garnish" are not included in the nutritional information. When alternate choices or amounts of ingredients are given, or a range in the number of servings is shown, the ingredient, amount, or number of servings listed first has been used for analysis.

A WORD ABOUT KIDS

Like many American adults, too many children are also over-weight, obese, and diabetic. Today, children as young as 10 years old are being diagnosed with Type 2 diabetes, which used to be thought of as a disease of older adults. But with a poor diet and inactive lifestyle, children, too, are developing diabetes.

By following a healthy eating plan and increasing physical activity, children can lose weight and control diabetes. At the same time, they need not feel that they are different and must eat foods other than those eaten by their family and friends.

Many of the recipes in *Diabetes Snacks, Treats & Easy Eats* will appeal to children, with or without diabetes. Be sure to check with your child's doctor, registered dietitian, or certified diabetes educator to pick the recipes that will fit into your child's individualized meal plan. Then serve the recipes with confidence to your entire family, knowing that everyone can enjoy familiar and delicious food together. After all, it's about sensible eating, portion control, and exercising daily. It's not about "good," "bad," or "forbidden" foods.

ENJOY YOURSELF

Even though you may have diabetes, you can see that with a little knowledge and effort you can eat delicious food, enjoy meals with family and friends, and take steps to control your blood glucose— and your diabetes.

SHOPPING & PANTRY TIPS

Take some time at the supermarket to choose products wisely. The good news is that there are many more new items suitable and adaptable for people with diabetes than ever before. I often wish that my mother could have sampled these new products when she fought diabetes in the days before low-fat alternatives and sugar substitutes.

While there are an enormous number of fat-free, sugar-free, and low-cholesterol snacks and other products available, be aware that many of them still have a lot of calories and might be higher in sugar, carbs, or starches than their full-fat counterparts. Also, even a "free," low-calorie, low-fat, no-sugar-added food can add up in calories, fat, sodium, or carbs if you exceed the recommended serving size.

Always have a selection of nonstick cooking sprays on hand. The favorites in my house are olive oil and butter flavors. Use the sprays according to the directions.

You may also wish to keep a variety of sugar substitutes in your pantry to help sweeten foods without raising the calorie or carb count. However, small amounts of sugar are allowed, especially in baked goods, where sugar is necessary for rising and texture. Some recipes work very well with a combination of a small amount of sugar and sugar substitute.

I also keep reduced-fat margarine on hand. You will need both tub and stick varieties. While tub margarines have fewer unhealthful trans-fatty acids, for baking and cooking you'll need regular stick reduced-fat margarine.

Canola oil is a good all-purpose oil to keep on hand in the pantry. It is rich in health-protective Omega-3 fatty acids. Canola oil also has the lowest percentage of saturated fat of any vegetable oil. Saturated fat interferes with the normal removal of excess fat and cholesterol from the body.

Always buy the highest quality spices and extracts and the freshest herbs available. Extracts such as vanilla, chocolate, anise, and maple flavoring and herbs such as cilantro and rosemary provide wonderful flavor without adding calories or carbs.

Sugar-free, fat-free whipped toppings add sweet flavor and creamy texture to desserts, both as a topping and as an ingredient, for instance, in pie fillings. Numerous flavors of sugar-free instant puddings also are available, as are sugar-free gelatin desserts.

If eggs fit into your eating plan, look for brands with added Omega-3 fatty acids. To cut the amount of fat and cholesterol in recipes containing eggs, you may wish to substitute egg whites for some of the yolks. Egg-white omelets are my family's favorite. Or you can use the new fat-free, cholesterol-free liquid egg substitutes.

Always use nonfat or reduced-fat dairy products, such as milk, buttermilk, cottage cheese, yogurt, sour cream, and cheese, instead of their full-fat counterparts.

Always skin poultry and cut or trim away with kitchen shears any visible fat on any meat. Always use lean cuts of meat and extra-lean ground meats.

To sweeten the morning, try this easy cinnamon topping: Mix 3 to 4 packets of sugar substitute with 2 teaspoons cinnamon. Whether you are watching your sugar intake or not, this is a good topping to have on hand for sprinkling over cut grapefruit, toast, or cereals.

While no-sugar-added fruit spreads are available, use them in moderation because the carbohydrate and calorie counts are nearly the same as for regular jams and preserves.

CHAPTER ONE

Snacks

Substitute your favorite cereal, nuts, and dried fruit to make this a special treat.

◇ **LOW SODIUM**

TRAIL MIX

MAKES 4 CUPS, OR 8 (½-CUP) SERVINGS

1 ½ cups corn, rice, or oat cereal

1 cup sliced almonds or shelled pistachios

½ cup chopped dried fruit, such as apricots, pineapple, apples, or pears

½ cup dried raisins or currants

Toss together the cereal, nuts, dried fruit, and raisins or currants in a mixing bowl.

Divide the mix into individual portions and place in small self-sealing food storage bags. Keep in a cool, dry place.

Per Serving: Calories: 166; % Calories from fat: 42; Fat (gm): 8.3; Saturated fat (gm): 0.6; Cholesterol (mg): 0; Sodium (mg): 24; Protein (gm): 4.4; Carbohydrate (gm): 21.3
Exchanges: Milk: 0.0; Vegetable: 0.0; Fruit: 1.0; Bread: 1.0; Meat: 0.0; Fat: 1.5

Conventional ranch-style dressing is loaded with fat and calories. Our version, made with dry ranch-style dressing mix and yogurt, is a much healthier alternative.

🐮 LOW FAT

CARROT AND CELERY STICKS WITH RANCH DIP

MAKES 4 SERVINGS, ¼ CUP DRESSING AND 1 CUP VEGETABLES PER SERVING

1 package (1 ounce) dry ranch-style dressing mix
1 cup nonfat plain yogurt
2 cups carrot sticks or baby carrots
2 cups celery sticks

Stir together the dressing mix with the yogurt in a small bowl. Cover and refrigerate until ready to serve.

At serving time, arrange the carrot and celery sticks on a dish. Serve with the dip.

Per Serving: Calories: 86; % Calories from fat: 3; Fat (gm): 0.3; Saturated fat (gm): 0.1; Cholesterol (mg): 1.2; Sodium (mg): 156; Protein (gm): 4.6; Carbohydrate (gm): 17
Exchanges: Milk: 0.0; Vegetable: 3.0; Fruit: 0.0; Bread: 0.0; Meat: 0.0; Fat: 0.0

Freezing grapes yields a simple grape "sherbet" that is a delicious, healthful snack. Serve the grapes as soon as they are frozen. Grapes can be frozen in bunches or individually.

⚬ **LOW CARB**
🐄 **LOW FAT**
◇ **LOW SODIUM**

ICED GRAPES

MAKES 8 (½-CUP) SERVINGS

1 pound seedless green or red grapes

Wash and dry grapes. Set grapes on a plate or put them in a plastic self-sealing bag. Freeze for 2 to 3 hours.

Serve frozen.

Per Serving: Calories: 40; % Calories from fat: 7; Fat (gm): 0.3; Saturated fat (gm): 0.1; Cholesterol (mg): O; Sodium (mg): 1; Protein (gm): 0.4; Carbohydrate (gm): 10.1
Exchanges: Milk: 0.0; Vegetable: 0.0; Fruit: 1.0; Bread: 0.0; Meat: 0.0; Fat: 0.0

For a single serving and faster preparation, place one serving in a glass pie plate without the aluminum foil and microwave on HIGH 30 seconds or until cheese melts.

◔ LOW CARB

TORTILLA MELT

MAKES 6 SERVINGS, 4 CHIPS PER SERVING

24 tortilla chips
$1/2$ cup shredded low-fat mozzarella cheese
$1/3$ cup jarred salsa or homemade (see recipe Page 109)

Preheat oven to 400 degrees F. Arrange tortilla chips on a baking sheet lined with aluminum foil.

Sprinkle tortillas with cheese and salsa. Bake a few minutes or until hot and cheese melts.

Per Serving: Calories: 93; % Calories from fat: 40; Fat (gm): 4.3; Saturated fat (gm): 1.1; Cholesterol (mg): 0.8; Sodium (mg): 149; Protein (gm): 3.8; Carbohydrate (gm): 10.5
Exchanges: Milk: 0.0; Vegetable: 1.0; Fruit: 0.0; Bread: 0.5; Meat: 0.0; Fat: 1.0

Most commercially prepared popcorns are loaded with fat, salt, and artificial flavors. To keep fat and salt to a minimum, buy top quality popcorn that doesn't need lots of butter and salt for flavor. Prepared properly at home, popcorn is low in fat and high in fiber, making it a healthier alternative to potato chips and other fatty, salty snacks. If using an electric air popper, follow the manufacturer's directions. If you use a special microwave popper, follow those directions.

⭖ **LOW CARB**
🐄 **LOW FAT**

MICROWAVE POPCORN

MAKES 2 (1-CUP) SERVINGS

- 2 tablespoons unpopped popcorn kernels
- 1 medium brown paper bag without printing
- ¼ teaspoon salt or a flavored salt, such as Parmesan/garlic or barbecue

Place the kernels in the paper bag and seal the bag tightly by rolling up the top.

Microwave on HIGH for 3 minutes or until the popping slows down to occasional pops. The timing may vary depending on the wattage of your microwave.

Remove the bag from the microwave and pour the corn into a bowl Season with salt.

SERVING SUGGESTIONS: Drizzle a tablespoon of melted reduced-fat margarine over the popped corn, sprinkle the popped corn with a small amount of cinnamon sugar, which can be made by mixing together 2 teaspoons ground cinnamon and 2 to 3 packets of sugar substitute, or add raisins and sunflower seeds to the popped corn and toss.

....

Per Serving: Calories: 30; % Calories from fat: 9; Fat (gm): 0.3; Saturated fat (gm): 0; Cholesterol (mg): 0; Sodium (mg): 291; Protein (gm): 0.9; Carbohydrate (gm): 6.1
Exchanges: Milk: 0.0; Vegetable: 0.0; Fruit: 0.0; Bread: 0.5; Meat: 0.0; Fat: 0.0

Nachos can be served as an after-school snack, as a quick lunch, or as party food. Add garlic powder or a chopped jalapeño pepper for a spicier flavor.

NACHOS

MAKES 8 SERVINGS, 7 CHIPS PER SERVING

- 56 baked tortilla chips (4 ounces)
  Olive oil-flavored nonstick cooking spray
- 1 cup chopped green onions
- 2 1/2 teaspoons chili powder
- 6 ounces ground turkey
- 1 can (14 1/2 ounces) Mexican-style diced tomatoes, drained
- 1 cup (4 ounces) shredded reduced-fat Monterey jack cheese

Preheat oven to 350 degrees F. Spread the chips on a baking sheet.

Heat a large nonstick frying pan lightly coated with cooking spray over medium heat. Add onions and chili powder. Cook for a few minutes until onions are translucent and tender, stirring and spraying once. Stir in turkey. Continue cooking until no longer pink. Stir in the tomatoes.

Spoon the tomato mixture over the chips and sprinkle with cheese. Bake 5 minutes or until cheese melts.

TIP: Substitute ground chicken, beef, or pork for the ground turkey.

Per Serving: Calories: 148; % Calories from fat: 34; Fat (gm): 5.9; Saturated fat (gm): 2.5; Cholesterol (mg): 26.8; Sodium (mg): 308; Protein (gm): 9.4; Carbohydrate (gm): 16
Exchanges: Milk: 0.0; Vegetable: 0.0; Fruit: 0.0; Bread: 1.0; Meat: 1.0; Fat: 0.5

This snack is quick and easy to make and packs well in a school lunch.

◌ **LOW CARB**
🐮 **LOW FAT**

ANTS ON A LOG

MAKES 4 SERVINGS, 1 STALK CELERY PER SERVING

$^1/_2$ cup low-fat small curd cottage cheese or reduced-fat cream cheese

1 to 2 tablespoons skim milk

2 tablespoons mashed banana

4 stalks celery, cut in 3-inch pieces

$^1/_4$ cup raisins or currants

Mix the cheese, milk, and banana together in a small bowl.

Spoon the filling into the cut celery sticks. Gently press the raisins on top of the cheese.

Cover and refrigerate until ready to serve.

Per Serving: Calories: 41; % Calories from fat: 14; Fat (gm): 0.6; Saturated fat (gm): 0.4; Cholesterol (mg): 2.3; Sodium (mg): 152; Protein (gm): 4.5; Carbohydrate (gm): 4.7
Exchanges: Milk: 0.0; Vegetable: 1.0; Fruit: 0.0; Bread: 0.0; Meat: 0.0; Fat: 0.0

Using reduced-fat cottage cheese and nonfat salad dressing instead of traditional mayonnaise means deviled eggs don't have to come off your menu.

◔ **LOW CARB**
🔥 **LOW FAT**
◇ **LOW SODIUM**

DEVILED EGGS

MAKES 12 EGG HALVES, 1 EGG HALF PER SERVING

> 6 large eggs
> 1/4 cup reduced-fat or fat-free cottage cheese
> 3 tablespoons nonfat ranch-style dressing
> 1 teaspoon prepared mustard
> 2 tablespoons finely chopped green pepper

Place eggs in a saucepan and cover with water. Bring to a boil over medium heat. Remove saucepan from heat. Let eggs stand in pan, covered, for 20 minutes. Drain. Cool eggs and peel.

Slice eggs lengthwise and remove the yolks. Arrange the whites, cut side up, on a plate and cover with plastic wrap until ready to fill.

Combine the cottage cheese, dressing, mustard, and yolks. Mash with a fork until smooth. Mix in the green pepper. Spoon the filling into the egg whites.

Cover and keep cold until ready to serve.

SERVING SUGGESTION: Add 2 tablespoons of chopped fresh parsley or dill or 1/2 teaspoon curry powder to the filling for extra flavor.

Per Serving: Calories: 48; % Calories from fat: 50; Fat (gm): 2.6; Saturated fat (gm): 0.8; Cholesterol (mg): 106.4; Sodium (mg): 99; Protein (gm): 3.7; Carbohydrate (gm): 1.9
Exchanges: Milk: 0.0; Vegetable: 0.0; Fruit: 0.0; Bread: 0.0; Meat: 0.5; Fat: 0.5

Nothing beats the heat faster than ice-cold watermelon. Serve this luscious smoothie on one of those "dog days" of summer.

⦿ **LOW CARB**
⦿ **LOW FAT**
⬦ **LOW SODIUM**

WATERMELON SMOOTHIE

MAKES 2 SERVINGS, ABOUT 1½ CUPS PER SERVING

2 to 4 ice cubes or ½ cup crushed ice

3 cups cubed and frozen seedless watermelon

Lemon slices, optional

If using ice cubes, crush the ice in a blender on high speed. Add the watermelon and liquefy. If using crushed ice, add ice and watermelon to blender together and liquefy.

Pour smoothie into 2 tall glasses and garnish with lemon if desired.

Per Serving: Calories: 54; % Calories from fat: 11; Fat (gm): 0.7; Saturated fat (gm): 0.1; Cholesterol (mg): 0; Sodium (mg): 3; Protein (gm): 1.1; Carbohydrate (gm): 12.2
Exchanges: Milk: 0.0; Vegetable: 0.0; Fruit: 1.0; Bread: 0.0; Meat: 0.0; Fat: 0.0

As a time-saver, microwave the onion rings instead of steaming. To microwave, cover loosely with plastic wrap and microwave on HIGH for 1 to 2 minutes or until the onions are tender.

🐮 LOW FAT
◇ LOW SODIUM

BAKED ONION RINGS

MAKES 8 SERVINGS

1 to 2 large onions, peeled, sliced, and separated into rings
$\frac{1}{2}$ cup egg substitute
$\frac{1}{2}$ cup yellow corn grits or coarse cornmeal
$\frac{1}{2}$ cup all-purpose flour
$\frac{1}{4}$ teaspoon salt
$\frac{1}{8}$ teaspoon black pepper
Olive oil-flavored nonstick cooking spray

Preheat oven to 400 degrees F. Steam the onion rings in a covered saucepan with a little water for 6 to 7 minutes. Drain and cool.

Pour egg substitute into a shallow bowl. Toss onion rings with eggs. In a separate bowl, mix together the grits, flour, salt, and pepper. Coat onion rings with flour mixture.

Lightly coat a nonstick baking sheet with cooking spray. Arrange onion rings on baking sheet.

Bake 10 to 12 minutes. Turn rings over and continue baking for 6 minutes or until crisp.

Per Serving: Calories: 95; % Calories from fat: 3; Fat (gm): 0.3; Saturated fat (gm): 0; Cholesterol (mg): 0; Sodium (mg): 103; Protein (gm): 3.9; Carbohydrate (gm): 19.2
Exchanges: Milk: 0.0; Vegetable: 1.0; Fruit: 0.0; Bread: 1.0; Meat: 0.0; Fat: 0.5

Oven-fried sweet potato wedges make a delicious and healthful alternative to traditional French fries.

☺ **LOW FAT**
◇ **LOW SODIUM**

SWEET POTATO WEDGES

MAKES 4 SERVINGS, 6 WEDGES PER SERVING

4 medium sweet potatoes, washed and cut lengthwise into 6 wedges

Olive oil-flavored cooking spray

Salt, to taste

$1/8$ teaspoon black pepper

$1/4$ teaspoon garlic powder

1 cup Chunky Salsa (see recipe Page 109) or store-bought

Preheat oven to 450 degrees F. Lightly coat baking sheet with olive oil flavored nonstick cooking spray.

Soak potato wedges in cold water to cover for 10 minutes, then drain. Pat dry with paper towels.

Lightly coat potato wedges with cooking spray, then sprinkle with salt, black pepper, and garlic powder. Arrange wedges in a single layer on baking sheet.

Bake potatoes about 45 minutes or until browned, crisp, and fork-tender, turning twice. Serve immediately with salsa for dipping.

Per Serving: Calories: 149; % Calories from fat: 3; Fat (gm): 0.5; Saturated fat (gm): 0.1; Cholesterol (mg): 0; Sodium (mg): 19; Protein (gm): 2.6; Carbohydrate (gm): 34.5
Exchanges: Milk: 0.0; Vegetable: 0.0; Fruit: 0.0; Bread: 2.0; Meat: 0.0; Fat: 0.0

CHAPTER TWO

Starters

TWO-BEAN SPREAD

MAKES 2 CUPS, OR 8 (¼-CUP) SERVINGS

- 2 cloves garlic, minced
- 1 can (15 ounces) cannellini beans, drained and rinsed (see note)
- 1 cup cooked chickpeas (garbanzos), drained and rinsed
- 3 tablespoons orange juice
- 2 tablespoons extra-virgin olive oil
- 1 tablespoon fresh lemon juice
  Salt, to taste
- ⅛ teaspoon black pepper
- ¼ teaspoon dried basil

Blend garlic, beans, chickpeas, orange juice, oil, lemon juice, salt, pepper, and basil until smooth in food processor, or mash together in a bowl with a potato masher.

Spoon mixture into a serving bowl and garnish with parsley sprig or paprika if desired.

NOTE: Cannellini beans are large white Italian kidney beans. Other white beans, such as Great Northern, can be substituted. To lower sodium in recipes, use reduced-sodium canned beans or cook your beans from scratch without salt.

Per Serving: Calories: 111; % Calories from fat: 32; Fat (gm): 3.9; Saturated fat (gm): 0.5; Cholesterol (mg): 0; Sodium (mg): 200; Protein (gm): 3.6; Carbohydrate (gm): 15.2
Exchanges: Milk: 0.0; Vegetable: 0.0; Fruit: 0.0; Bread: 1.0; Meat: 0.0; Fat: 1.0

*To reheat pita chips, preheat the oven to 250 degrees F., wrap
the chips in foil, and heat the chips for 12 to 15 minutes.*

PITA CHIPS

MAKES 24 CHIPS, OR 8 SERVINGS (3 CHIPS PER SERVING)

Olive-oil flavored cooking spray
4 whole-wheat pita bread pockets
1 teaspoon garlic powder

Preheat oven to 350 degrees F. Lightly coat a nonstick baking
sheet with cooking spray.

Cut each pita in half, then cut each half into 3 wedges. Set pita
wedges on prepared baking sheet. Lightly spray the wedges and
sprinkle with garlic powder.

Bake the wedges in the center of the oven for 7 minutes or until
lightly toasted.

Mound the chips into a serving basket or bowl and serve immediately. Cooled chips can be stored in an airtight container in a
cool, dry place and reheated as needed.

Per Serving: Calories: 86; % Calories from fat: 8; Fat (gm): 0.8; Saturated fat (gm): 0.1;
Cholesterol (mg): 0; Sodium (mg): 170; Protein (gm): 3.2; Carbohydrate (gm): 17.9
Exchanges: Milk: 0.0; Vegetable: 0.0; Fruit: 0.0; Bread: 1.0; Meat: 0.0; Fat: 0.0

Serve this dip with warm whole-wheat pita halves and cut up vegetables for dipping.

⏣ **LOW CARB**
♨ **LOW FAT**
◇ **LOW SODIUM**

EGGPLANT DIP

MAKES 3 CUPS, OR 6 ($\frac{1}{2}$-CUP) SERVINGS

> 1 large purple eggplant
> 1 can (14 $\frac{1}{2}$ ounces) diced tomatoes, drained
> $\frac{1}{2}$ cup chopped onion
> $\frac{1}{2}$ cup chopped parsley
> 2 tablespoons red wine vinegar
> 1 tablespoon olive oil
> $\frac{1}{4}$ teaspoon garlic powder or dried oregano
>   Salt, to taste
> $\frac{1}{8}$ teaspoon black pepper

Preheat oven to 375 degrees F. Place eggplant on baking sheet. Bake for 1 hour, turning occasionally, or until fork tender.

Remove eggplant from oven and cool on baking sheet. Cut lengthwise and scoop out pulp into mixing bowl. Discard skin. Mash pulp with a fork.

Stir in tomato, onion, parsley, vinegar, oil, garlic powder, salt, and pepper. Cover and refrigerate for 1 hour. Stir dip before serving.

Per Serving: Calories: 65; % Calories from fat: 33; Fat (gm): 2.5; Saturated fat (gm): 0.3; Cholesterol (mg): 0; Sodium (mg): 114; Protein (gm): 1.8; Carbohydrate (gm): 9.4
Exchanges: Milk: 0.0; Vegetable: 2.0; Fruit: 0.0; Bread: 0.0; Meat: 0.0; Fat: 0.5

Chinese pot stickers are small, bite-sized pastries with savory fillings. They are a snap to make with purchased wonton wrappers. The wrappers are available in the refrigerated produce section of most supermarkets.

🔥 **LOW CARB**
🐮 **LOW FAT**
◇ **LOW SODIUM**

VEGETABLE POT STICKERS

MAKES 24 POT STICKERS, OR 8 SERVINGS OF 3 POT STICKERS

Butter-flavored cooking spray
$1/_2$ cup chopped green onions
2 cups cleaned, chopped white mushrooms
Salt, to taste
$1/_8$ teaspoon black pepper
24 wonton wrappers (see note)
1 egg white, lightly beaten
2 tablespoons reduced-fat margarine

Lightly coat a nonstick frying pan with cooking spray. Add onions and mushrooms and cook over medium-high heat, stirring occasionally until tender, about 5 minutes. Season with salt and pepper. Cool and drain.

To assemble pot stickers, place 1 scant tablespoon of filling in the center of each wonton wrapper. Brush edges of wrapper with egg white. Fold wrapper in half, making a triangular shape. Press along edges, sealing dough.

Lightly coat a nonstick frying pan with cooking spray. Melt the margarine over medium heat. Fry the pot stickers until barely golden, turning once.

NOTE: Traditional wonton wrappers are thin dough squares about $3^1/_2$ by $3^1/_2$ inches. Round pot stickers are called gyoza. You might also find in the refrigerated section packages of wonton skins or egg roll wrappers in different sizes. All of these packaged doughs can be used to make pot stickers and wontons. Use a sharp knife or a cookie cutter to cut the dough to the size or shape you desire.

Per Serving: Calories: 73; % Calories from fat: 21; Fat (gm): 1.7; Saturated fat (gm): 0.3; Cholesterol (mg): 2.2; Sodium (mg): 97.4; Protein (gm): 2.6; Carbohydrate (gm): 2.3
Exchanges: Milk: 0.0; Vegetable: 1.0; Fruit: 0.0; Bread: 0.5; Meat: 0.0; Fat: 0.0

This is a good sauce to have on hand for pot stickers, wontons, and egg rolls.

◌ **LOW CARB**
🐄 **LOW FAT**
◇ **LOW SODIUM**

SWEET SAUCE

MAKES 2/3 CUP SAUCE, 1 TABLESPOON PER SERVING

$1/2$ cup no-added-sugar apricot fruit spread
2 tablespoons red wine vinegar
2 tablespoons water

Combine the fruit spread, vinegar, and water in a small saucepan. Cook over medium heat until blended, stirring often.

Cool and pour into a serving dish. Cover and refrigerate until ready to serve.

Per Serving: Calories: 30; % Calories from fat: 0; Fat (gm): 0; Saturated fat (gm): 0; Cholesterol (mg): 0; Sodium (mg): 0; Protein (gm): 0; Carbohydrate (gm): 7.5
Exchanges: Milk: 0.0; Vegetable: 0.0; Fruit: 0.0; Bread: 0.5; Meat: 0.0; Fat: 0.0

Traditional Crab Rangoon Wontons are deep-fried. Our healthier version is prepared like pot stickers in boiling water. For extra flavor, boil the wontons in low-sodium broth and add ½ teaspoon curry powder to the crab filling.

⚪ LOW CARB
🐖 LOW FAT

CRAB RANGOON WONTONS

MAKES 24 WONTONS, OR 8 SERVINGS OF 3 WONTONS

- ½ cup reduced-fat cream cheese
- ½ cup nonfat cottage cheese
- ¼ cup shredded crabmeat or crabmeat substitute
- 24 wonton wrappers (see note)
- 1 egg white, lightly beaten
- Nonstick cooking spray

Mix together the cream cheese and cottage cheese in a small bowl. Stir in crabmeat.

To assemble wontons, set 1 scant tablespoon of filling in the center of each wonton wrapper. Brush edges of wrapper with egg white. Fold wrapper in half, making a triangular shape, and press along edges, sealing dough. Set wontons on lightly floured nonstick cookie sheet until they are all assembled. Cover with plastic wrap to prevent drying.

Lightly coat a serving platter with cooking spray. Set aside, keeping warm.

Fill a medium saucepan half full of water. Bring to a boil. Slide half of the wontons into water. Cook 1½ to 2 minutes or until wontons are tender. Remove wontons with a slotted spoon and place on platter, keeping warm. Repeat until all of the wontons are cooked.

NOTE: Traditional wonton wrappers are dough squares about 3 1/2 by 3 1/2 inches. Round pot stickers are called gyoza. You might also find in the refrigerated section packages of wonton skins or egg roll wrappers in different sizes. All of these packaged doughs can be used to make pot stickers and wontons. Use a sharp knife or a cookie cutter to cut the dough to the size or shape you desire.

Per Serving: Calories: 100; % Calories from fat: 26; Fat (gm): 2.8; Saturated fat (gm): 1.8; Cholesterol (mg): 11.6; Sodium (mg): 216; Protein (gm): 5.5; Carbohydrate (gm): 12.5
Exchanges: Milk: 0.0; Vegetable: 0.0; Fruit: 0.0; Bread: 1.0; Meat: 0.0; Fat: 0.5

Tortillas and wraps come in a variety of flavors, including dried tomato, spinach, and whole-wheat. Experiment with flavors to find out what you like best. For extra flavor, season the wrap filling with dried oregano and alfalfa sprouts.

⏀ **LOW CARB**
☸ **LOW FAT**
◇ **LOW SODIUM**

CALIFORNIA WRAPS

MAKES 20 SLICES, 1 SLICE PER SERVING

- 1 cup reduced-fat ricotta cheese
- 2 (11-inch) whole-wheat flour tortillas or spinach wraps
- 1 large tomato, thinly sliced
- 2 cups washed, torn spinach or lettuce leaves
- 1 cup chopped onion
- 4 ounces thinly sliced roasted turkey breast

Spread $1/2$ cup of cheese evenly over each tortilla to within $1/4$ inch of the edge. Starting 1 inch from the bottom edge, layer the tomato, spinach, onion, and turkey over the cheese.

Starting from the bottom, roll up the wraps jelly-roll style. Wrap tightly in plastic wrap and refrigerate for 1 hour.

To serve, remove the plastic wrap and cut each roll on the diagonal into 1-inch slices.

Per Serving: Calories: 31; % Calories from fat: 13; Fat (gm): 0.5; Saturated fat (gm): 0.2; Cholesterol (mg): 6.9; Sodium (mg): 45; Protein (gm): 4; Carbohydrate (gm): 2.7
Exchanges: Milk: 0.0; Vegetable: 0.0; Fruit: 0.0; Bread: 0.0; Meat: 0.5; Fat: 0.0

Filo, a Greek pastry dough also spelled phyllo, is easy to work with and relatively low in calories, fat, and carbohydrates. It makes elegant-looking desserts and is readily available in the frozen-foods section of most supermarkets. When working with filo, cover it with a damp tea towel or plastic wrap to prevent drying and cracking.

SPINACH IN FILO

MAKES 4 SERVINGS

Olive oil-flavored nonstick cooking spray
- 1/2 cup chopped onion
- 1/2 cup thawed chopped spinach
- 2 tablespoons ricotta cheese
- 8 sheets thawed filo pastry

Butter-flavored nonstick cooking spray

Position rack in center of oven and preheat oven to 375 degrees F. Lightly coat a frying pan with olive oil-flavored cooking spray and heat over medium heat. Cook onion until translucent and tender, stirring several times and spraying once. Add spinach and cook until most moisture has evaporated. Remove pan from heat and stir in cheese.

Lightly coat 4 ceramic or glass custard cups with butter-flavored cooking spray. Lightly coat each filo sheet with butter-flavored cooking spray. Stack and cut sheets in half.

Working with 4 sheets at a time, shape filo to line each cup. Spoon in filling, and fold the filo over the top of each cup. Set cups on a baking sheet. Bake for 10 to 15 minutes or until filo is golden brown.

....

Per Serving: Calories: 155; % Calories from fat: 25; Fat (gm): 4.4; Saturated fat (gm): 1.8; Cholesterol (mg): 7.8; Sodium (mg): 217; Protein (gm): 5.4; Carbohydrate (gm): 23.4
Exchanges: Milk: 0.0; Vegetable: 0.0; Fruit: 0.0; Bread: 1.5; Meat: 0.0; Fat: 1.0

Save the potato flesh scooped from the skins and mix it with nonfat sour cream to serve as a snack or side dish the next day.

⏣ **LOW CARB**
🐮 **LOW FAT**
◈ **LOW SODIUM**

POTATO SKINS

MAKES 4 SERVINGS, 4 QUARTERS PER SERVING

> 4 medium-small (6 to 7 ounces each) baking potatoes, skin on
> Butter-flavored nonstick cooking spray
> 1 teaspoon garlic powder

Preheat oven to 450 degrees F. Pierce the potatoes in several places with the tip of a small knife. Lightly coat potatoes with cooking spray. Bake potatoes in the center of the oven for 30 minutes or until fork tender.

When potatoes are cool enough to handle, cut into quarters and scoop out the flesh with a teaspoon, leaving ¼ inch of potato flesh on the skin. Lightly coat the skins with cooking spray. Sprinkle with garlic powder.

Set skins on a nonstick baking sheet and return to the oven for 10 minutes, turning once, or until hot and crisp.

SERVING SUGGESTIONS: Garnish with nonfat yogurt and/or chopped green onions if desired.

Per Serving: Calories: 24; % Calories from fat: 1; Fat (gm): 0; Saturated fat (gm): 0; Cholesterol (mg): 0; Sodium (mg): 4; Protein (gm): 1.1; Carbohydrate (gm): 5.2
Exchanges: Milk: 0.0; Vegetable: 0.0; Fruit: 0.0; Bread: 0.5; Meat: 0.0; Fat: 0.0

To quickly and easily seed a tomato, simply cut the tomato in half horizontally and gently squeeze the seeds out of the two halves.

⏻ **LOW CARB**
🐮 **LOW FAT**

CROSTINI

MAKES 4 SERVINGS, 1 SLICE PER SERVING

     Olive oil-flavored nonstick cooking spray

3 tablespoons minced onion

¹/₂ cup seeded and chopped tomato

¹/₈ teaspoon garlic powder

¹/₄ teaspoon dried oregano

4 slices French or Italian bread, toasted

2 tablespoons grated Parmesan cheese

Preheat oven to 400 degrees F. Lightly coat a small nonstick frying pan with cooking spray. Cook onions over medium-low heat, stirring several times and spraying once, until translucent and tender. Add tomatoes. Season mixture with garlic powder and oregano. Continue cooking for 2 to 3 minutes, stirring often.

Arrange bread on a nonstick baking sheet. Spread bread with tomato mixture. Sprinkle with cheese. Bake for 5 minutes.

Per Serving: Calories: 88; % Calories from fat: 16; Fat (gm): 1.6; Saturated fat (gm): 0.7; Cholesterol (mg): 2; Sodium (mg): 201; Protein (gm): 3.5; Carbohydrate (gm): 14.9
Exchanges: Milk: 0.0; Vegetable: 0.0; Fruit: 0.0; Bread: 1.0; Meat: 0.0; Fat: 0.5

PIZZA SHRIMP ROLL

MAKES 8 ROLLS, 1 ROLL PER SERVING

Olive oil-flavored nonstick cooking spray
1/2 pound cooked baby shrimp (about 1 cup)
1/2 cup chopped green onions
1 1/2 cups reduced-fat ricotta cheese
1 can (10 ounces) pizza crust dough or homemade

Lightly coat a baking sheet with cooking spray. Preheat oven to 425 degrees F.

Mix together in a small bowl the shrimp, onion, and ricotta cheese.

Roll out the dough into a rectangle on a lightly floured surface. Spread the filling over the dough. Roll up the dough, jelly-roll style, rolling the short end down to meet the other short end. Cut the roll into 8 equal pieces. Set each roll on the baking sheet, cut side up.

Cover rolls with aluminum foil or a warm damp kitchen towel and let rise in a warm place for 30 to 35 minutes until nearly doubled in bulk.

Bake for 20 minutes or until the rolls are golden brown.

Per Serving: Calories: 168; % Calories from fat: 16; Fat (gm): 3; Saturated fat (gm): 1.2; Cholesterol (mg): 63.4; Sodium (mg): 333; Protein (gm): 15.9; Carbohydrate (gm): 19
Exchanges: Milk: 0.0; Vegetable: 0.0; Fruit: 0.0; Bread: 1.0; Meat: 2.0; Fat: 0.0

This flavorful, virtually fat-free dip is great served with celery or carrot sticks. If you serve with crackers, look for brands made with whole grains and no hydrogenated fats.

◊ LOW CARB
♨ LOW FAT
◊ LOW SODIUM

CARROT CHILI DIP

MAKES ABOUT 3 CUPS, OR 6 (½-CUP) SERVINGS

2 cups nonfat plain yogurt
½ cup finely diced carrot
½ cup finely diced yellow onion
2 teaspoons Dijon mustard
1 tablespoon mild chili power

Mix together yogurt, carrot, onion, mustard, and chili powder in a bowl. Cover and chill for flavors to blend.

When ready to serve, bring the dip to room temperature.

Per Serving: Calories: 61; % Calories from fat: 6; Fat (gm): 0.4; Saturated fat (gm): 0.1; Cholesterol (mg): 1.6; Sodium (mg): 118; Protein (gm): 5.1; Carbohydrate (gm): 9.2
Exchanges: Milk: 0.5; Vegetable: 0.0; Fruit: 0.0; Bread: 0.0; Meat: 0.0; Fat: 0.0

These egg rolls are great filled with vegetables. For company, add a cup of cooked baby shrimp, if you wish. If it fits into your food plan, serve the egg rolls with Sweet Sauce (see Page 19).

◇ **LOW SODIUM**

EGG ROLLS

MAKES 6 EGG ROLLS, 1 ROLL PER SERVING

Olive oil-flavored nonstick cooking spray
2 tablespoons canola oil
$1/3$ cup chopped green onions
$1/8$ teaspoon garlic powder
$1/8$ teaspoon salt
$1/8$ teaspoon black pepper
3 cups shredded cabbage
2 cups bean sprouts, washed and drained
6 egg roll wrappers (see note)

Lightly coat a nonstick frying pan with cooking spray. Heat pan over medium-high heat. Add oil and onions. Season with garlic powder, salt, and black pepper. Add cabbage and bean sprouts and cook, stirring, until tender-crisp, about 3 minutes. Cool.

Place portion of filling in center of a wrapper. Fold up wrapper envelope style and seal, using water or egg white on edges. Repeat with remaining wrappers.

Spray a nonstick frying pan with olive oil-flavored nonstick cooking spray. Pan fry the egg rolls quickly, a few seconds on each of the four sides until a golden brown. Serve with Sweet Sauce if desired.

NOTE: Packages of egg roll wrapper dough, also called egg roll skins, are available in the refrigerated produce section of most supermarkets.

....

Per Serving: Calories: 119; % Calories from fat: 36; Fat (gm): 5; Saturated fat (gm): 0.4; Cholesterol (mg): 2.4; Sodium (mg): 118; Protein (gm): 3.4; Carbohydrate (gm): 16.5
Exchanges: Milk: 0.0; Vegetable: 0.0; Fruit: 1.0; Bread: 1.0; Meat: 0.0; Fat: 1.0

This dip is a version of hummus, a popular Middle Eastern dish. Chickpeas are also called garbanzo and ceci beans.

CHICKPEA DIP

MAKES 6 (¼ CUP) SERVINGS

1 tablespoon olive oil
1 can (16 ounces) chickpeas, rinsed and drained
2 tablespoons lemon juice
2 tablespoons reduced-fat peanut butter
1 tablespoon sesame seeds

Blend together in a food processor or blender the oil, chickpeas, lemon juice, and peanut butter, scraping down the sides of the bowl or jar as necessary.

Spoon into a serving bowl and sprinkle with sesame seeds.

SERVING SUGGESTION: Serve with cut-up vegetables or whole-wheat pita bread cut into triangles. If desired, add a little cayenne pepper to the dip for extra zip.

Per Serving: Calories: 151; % Calories from fat: 34; Fat (gm): 5.8; Saturated fat (gm): 0.9; Cholesterol (mg): 0; Sodium (mg): 258; Protein (gm): 5.2; Carbohydrate (gm): 20.4
Exchanges: Milk: 0.0; Vegetable: 0.0; Fruit: 0.0; Bread: 1.5; Meat: 0.0; Fat: 1.0

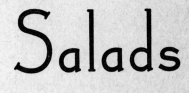

CHAPTER THREE

Salads

For faster preparation and less waste, purchase packaged shredded cabbage, which can be found in the produce section of most supermarkets.

⚬ **LOW CARB**
🐄 **LOW FAT**

COLESLAW

MAKES 12 (¾-CUP) SERVINGS

   6 cups shredded green cabbage
   2 cups grated carrots
   ¾ cup fat-free mayonnaise
   ¼ cup red wine vinegar
   3 tablespoons sugar or spoonable sugar substitute
   ¼ teaspoon salt
   ½ teaspoon black pepper
   ½ teaspoon dry mustard

Toss together the cabbage and carrots in large bowl.

Whisk together the mayonnaise, vinegar, sugar, salt, black pepper, and mustard in a small bowl. Toss the dressing with the vegetables.

Serve immediately or cover with plastic wrap and refrigerate until serving time. Toss coleslaw again before serving.

SERVING SUGGESTION: Substitute half of the green cabbage with shredded red cabbage. For extra flavor, add ½ cup sliced red onion and 1 tablespoon celery seeds.

Per Serving: Calories: 39; % Calories from fat: 4; Fat (gm): 0.2; Saturated fat (gm): 0; Cholesterol (mg): 0; Sodium (mg): 181; Protein (gm): 0.7; Carbohydrate (gm): 8.8
Exchanges: Milk: 0.0; Vegetable: 2.0; Fruit: 0.0; Bread: 0.0; Meat: 0.0; Fat: 0.0

Chopped parsley or dill sprigs make a nice garnish for this salad. To vary the salad, add two chopped hard-boiled eggs and 1/2 cup chopped green onions.

☻ LOW FAT

POTATO SALAD

MAKES 8 (1-CUP) SERVINGS

1 1/2 pounds red potatoes (about 5 medium potatoes)
1/3 cup fat-free mayonnaise or fat-free sandwich spread
1/2 cup chopped celery
1/4 teaspoon salt
1/8 teaspoon black pepper

Cover the potatoes with cold water in a large saucepan and bring to a boil. Reduce heat and simmer until the potatoes are fork-tender, about 15 to 20 minutes. Drain the potatoes and let stand until cool enough to handle.

Cut potatoes into cubes. Mix together the potatoes, mayonnaise, celery, salt, and black pepper in a large mixing bowl.

Cover and refrigerate until ready to serve. Toss before serving.

Per Serving: Calories: 68; % Calories from fat: 0; Fat (gm): 0; Saturated fat (gm): 0; Cholesterol (mg): 0; Sodium (mg): 189; Protein (gm): 1.1; Carbohydrate (gm): 16.7
Exchanges: Milk: 0.0; Vegetable: 0.0; Fruit: 0.0; Bread: 1.0; Meat: 0.0; Fat: 0.0

In Italian, this salad is called panzanella, for the bread it is made with. The salad makes great use of leftover or day-old bread. If you do not have day-old bread on hand, tear a fresh loaf into pieces and place the pieces on a baking sheet in a 325°F. oven. Bake about 5 minutes or until the pieces are slightly dried and crispy.

⚬ LOW CARB
🐾 LOW FAT

ITALIAN BREAD AND TOMATO SALAD

MAKES 8 (2-CUP) SERVINGS

8 cups torn romaine lettuce
1 cup cannellini beans
1 ½ cups torn crusty Italian or peasant-style bread
1 ½ cups chopped fresh tomatoes
¾ cup sliced red onion
2 tablespoons sliced black olives, optional
½ cup calorie-free balsamic vinaigrette

Toss together the lettuce with the beans, bread, tomatoes, onions, olives, and vinaigrette.

Per Serving: Calories: 58; % Calories from fat: 8; Fat (gm): 0.6; Saturated fat (gm): 0.1; Cholesterol (mg): 0; Sodium (mg): 296; Protein (gm): 3; Carbohydrate (gm): 11
Exchanges: Milk: 0.0; Vegetable: 0.0; Fruit: 0.0; Bread: 1.0; Meat: 0.0; Fat: 0.0

Greek seasoning mix is available in the spice aisle of many supermarkets. To make your own, mix together $1/4$ cup dried oregano leaves, 2 tablespoons fennel seeds, 2 tablespoons crushed dried lemon grass, and $3/4$ teaspoon black peppercorns. Using a spice mill, electric coffee grinder, or mortar and pestle, grind spices to a fine powder. Store in a small glass jar.

◇ LOW SODIUM

GREEK ISLAND BEAN SALAD

MAKES 8 (1-CUP) SERVINGS

2 cans (15 ounces each) small white beans, rinsed and drained

$1/2$ cup grated carrots

$1/2$ cup cubed feta cheese

$1/2$ cup chopped cilantro

2 teaspoons Greek seasoning mix

$1/4$ cup lemon juice

3 tablespoons olive oil

Toss together the beans, carrots, cheese, cilantro, and seasoning mix.

Whisk together the lemon juice and olive oil in a small bowl. Stir into the bean mixture. Salad is best served at room temperature.

Per Serving: Calories: 199; % Calories from fat: 33; Fat (gm): 7.4; Saturated fat (gm): 2.1; Cholesterol (mg): 8.2; Sodium (mg): 111; Protein (gm): 9.2; Carbohydrate (gm): 25.1
Exchanges: Milk: 0.0; Vegetable: 0.0; Fruit: 0.0; Bread: 2.0; Meat: 0.0; Fat: 1.0

*Pay a visit to the salad bar in your favorite supermarket.
It is a convenient way to buy the "bits and pieces" or the
vegetables you need.*

Ò **LOW CARB**

GREEK SALAD

MAKES 8 (1½-CUP) SERVINGS

10 cups torn romaine lettuce
1 cup chopped fresh tomatoes
1 cup sliced red bell pepper
1 cup sliced cucumber
¼ cup sliced red onions
¼ cup cubed feta cheese
½ cup low-fat Greek-style salad dressing

Toss together the lettuce, tomatoes, bell pepper, cucumber,
onions, and cheese.

Add dressing and toss again.

Per Serving: Calories: 55; % Calories from fat: 50; Fat (gm): 3.5; Saturated fat (gm): 0.4;
Cholesterol (mg): 0.8; Sodium (mg): 140; Protein (gm): 1.7; Carbohydrate (gm): 6.1
Exchanges: Milk: 0.0; Vegetable: 1.0; Fruit: 0.0; Bread: 0.0; Meat: 0.0; Fat: 1.0

Taco salad gets a health update with our version made with turkey and garbanzo beans. If your eating plans allows, serve the salad with a few additional baked chips and a dollop of nonfat sour cream.

TACO SALAD

MAKES 6 (1½-CUP) SERVINGS

    Olive oil-flavored nonstick cooking spray
12 ounces lean ground turkey (about 1 cup)
 1 tablespoon mild chili powder
 8 cups torn Boston lettuce
 1 cup chopped tomatoes
 1 cup sliced cucumber
 1 cup garbanzo beans
12 baked nonfat tortilla chips, crumbled

Lightly coat a nonstick frying pan with cooking spray. Sprinkle the turkey with the chili powder and cook over medium heat, stirring and breaking up the turkey, for about 5 minutes or until the turkey is no longer pink.

Toss together the turkey, lettuce, tomatoes, cucumber, and garbanzo beans in a salad bowl. Sprinkle with tortilla chips before serving.

Per Serving: Calories: 195; % Calories from fat: 28; Fat (gm): 6.2; Saturated fat (gm): 1.5; Cholesterol (mg): 44.8; Sodium (mg): 236; Protein (gm): 14; Carbohydrate (gm): 21
Exchanges: Milk: 0.0; Vegetable: 1.0; Fruit: 0.0; Bread: 1.0; Meat: 2.0; Fat: 0.0

For a little more zing, add a few tablespoons of capers or chopped pickles and a dash of paprika. A half cup of fat-free mayonnaise can be substituted for the ranch-style dressing.

⌀ **LOW CARB**
🐮 **LOW FAT**

SALMON PASTA SALAD

MAKES 8 (¾-CUP) SERVINGS

2 cups cooked whole-wheat pasta shells
1 can (6 ½ ounces) salmon, drained
1 cup chopped celery
1 cup chopped red bell pepper
⅓ nonfat ranch-style dressing

Toss together the pasta, salmon, celery, and bell pepper in a salad bowl. Add dressing and toss again.

Per Serving: Calories: 100; % Calories from fat: 13; Fat (gm): 1.5; Saturated fat (gm): 0.4; Cholesterol (mg): 9; Sodium (mg): 243; Protein (gm): 7.1; Carbohydrate (gm): 14.7
Exchanges: Milk: 0.0; Vegetable: 0.0; Fruit: 0.0; Bread: 1.0; Meat: 0.5; Fat: 0.0

A sprinkling of chopped walnuts makes a nice garnish for this salad. Serve it on a plate lined with green lettuce leaves.

⟡ LOW CARB
🐮 LOW FAT

WALDORF CHICKEN SALAD

MAKES 4 (1-CUP) SERVINGS

- ¼ cup fat-free mayonnaise
- ¼ cup fat-free sour cream
- 2 cups cored, chopped apples, unpeeled
- 1 cup chopped celery
- ¾ cup chopped cooked skinless and boneless chicken, or turkey, breast

Mix together the mayonnaise and sour cream in a small bowl.

Toss apples with celery and chicken in mixing bowl. Add dressing and toss again.

Per Serving: Calories: 104; % Calories from fat: 9; Fat (gm): 1; Saturated fat (gm): 0.3; Cholesterol (mg): 20.2; Sodium (mg): 175; Protein (gm): 8.9; Carbohydrate (gm): 14.5
Exchanges: Milk: 0.0; Vegetable: 0.0; Fruit: 1.0; Bread: 0.0; Meat: 1.0; Fat: 0.0

CHAPTER FOUR

Soups
and
Stews

For a richer flavor, add 3 tablespoons low-sodium ketchup or pasta sauce. Ratatouille tastes even better the day after it is made, and it also makes a good pasta topper.

◔ **LOW CARB**
♨ **LOW FAT**

RATATOUILLE

MAKES 8 (2-CUP) SERVINGS

Olive oil-flavored nonstick cooking spray
1 cup chopped onion
1 large eggplant, chopped (about 4 cups)
2 cups sliced zucchini
2 cups chopped red bell peppers
1 can (14 $\frac{1}{2}$ ounces) low-sodium chopped tomatoes, including juice
$\frac{1}{2}$ cup fat-free Italian dressing

Lightly coat a nonstick frying pan with cooking spray. Cook the onion and eggplant over medium heat, stirring occasionally, until the onions are soft but not browned, about 3 minutes.

Stir in the zucchini, bell pepper, tomatoes, and juice. Add salad dressing. Cover and cook for 15 minutes. Uncover and cook, stirring occasionally, another 15 to 20 minutes.

Per Serving: Calories: 60; % Calories from fat: 4; Fat (gm): 0.3; Saturated fat (gm): 0; Cholesterol (mg): 0; Sodium (mg): 232; Protein (gm): 2; Carbohydrate (gm): 12.8
Exchanges: Milk: 0.0; Vegetable: 2.0; Fruit: 0.0; Bread: 0.0; Meat: 0.0; Fat: 0.0

This soup has some texture. If you prefer a smooth soup, cool the soup slightly and purée in a blender or food processor. Reheat the soup to serve.

⭘ **LOW CARB**
🐮 **LOW FAT**
◇ **LOW SODIUM**

PUMPKIN SOUP

MAKES 8 (1-CUP) SERVINGS

Butter-flavored nonstick cooking spray
1 ½ cups chopped red bell pepper
1 medium onion, chopped
1 can (29 ounces) pumpkin purée
1 can (28 ounces) low-sodium chicken broth
1 teaspoon pumpkin pie spice

Lightly coat a medium saucepan with cooking spray. Cook the onion and red pepper over medium heat for 5 minutes, stirring occasionally.

Stir in the pumpkin, broth, and spice mixture. Continue cooking for 20 minutes, partially covered.

Per Serving: Calories: 67; % Calories from fat: 12; Fat (gm): 1; Saturated fat (gm): 0.2; Cholesterol (mg): 10.3; Sodium (mg): 110; Protein (gm): 4.4; Carbohydrate (gm): 11.4
Exchanges: Milk: 0.0; Vegetable: 0.0; Fruit: 0.0; Bread: 1.0; Meat: 0.0; Fat: 0.0

*This recipe is delicious with a number of different fruits.
Try peaches, plums, or blueberries or a blend of fruits.
Garnish the soup with sliced strawberries or a dollop of
nonfat, sugar-free strawberry yogurt.*

⟡ **LOW CARB**
☙ **LOW FAT**
◇ **LOW SODIUM**

STRAWBERRY SOUP

MAKES 6 (1¼-CUP) SERVINGS

- 1 package (10 ounces) frozen, unsweetened strawberries, thawed
- 2 cups nonfat plain yogurt
- 1 quart sugar-free ginger ale

Using a blender or a food processor fitted with a steel blade,
process the strawberries until smooth. Add the yogurt and process
until smooth. Pour strawberry-yogurt mixture into large serving
pitcher. Stir in ginger ale.

Place covered pitcher in refrigerator and chill until ready to serve.

TIP: For a thicker soup, add additional nonfat plain yogurt.

Per Serving: Calories: 63; % Calories from fat: 6; Fat (gm): 0.5; Saturated fat (gm): 0.1;
Cholesterol (mg): 1.6; Sodium (mg): 105; Protein (gm): 5; Carbohydrate (gm): 10.7
Exchanges: Milk: 0.5; Vegetable: 0.0; Fruit: 0.5; Bread: 0.0; Meat: 0.0; Fat: 0.0

For special occasions, use a cleaned pumpkin as a soup tureen. The carved top of the pumpkin can serve as a lid to keep the soup warm. This soup and Pumpkin Soup (recipe on Page 43) lend themselves to being served in a pumpkin.

🐄 LOW FAT

ROOT VEGETABLE AND BARLEY SOUP

MAKES 8 (2-CUP) SERVINGS

- 1 tablespoon canola-blend oil
- 2 cups chopped onion
- 2 cups sliced parsnips
- 1 package (10 ounces) sliced carrots or 2 cups sliced carrots
- 1 can (48 ounces) low-sodium vegetable broth
- 2 cups cooked instant barley

Heat oil in a large nonstick soup pot. Cook onions, parsnips, and carrots over medium heat, stirring occasionally, for 4 to 5 minutes.

Add broth. Bring to a boil, reduce heat, and simmer.

Continue cooking, partially covered, for 45 minutes or until the vegetables are tender. Add the barley and cook until heated through.

Ladle soup into pumpkin, if using. Serve soup from pumpkin at the table.

Per Serving: Calories: 139; % Calories from fat: 16; Fat (gm): 2.5; Saturated fat (gm): 0.2; Cholesterol (mg): 0; Sodium (mg): 358; Protein (gm): 2.9; Carbohydrate (gm): 27.3
Exchanges: Milk: 0.0; Vegetable: 0.0; Fruit: 0.0; Bread: 2.0; Meat: 0.0; Fat: 0.0

This soup prepared without the noodles makes an excellent dish on its own, or it can be the base for other soups.

☺ LOW FAT

VEGETABLE SOUP WITH ALPHABET NOODLES

MAKES 8 (2-CUP) SERVINGS

    1 can (48 ounces) low-sodium, fat-free beef broth
    2 packages (1 pound each) soup vegetables
    1 cup sliced onion
    1/4 teaspoon salt
    1/4 teaspoon black pepper
    1/4 teaspoon dried thyme
    2 cups cooked alphabet noodles

In a large soup pot, bring to a boil the broth, vegetables, and onion. Reduce to a simmer.

Season with salt, pepper, and thyme. Partially cover and continue cooking for 10 minutes. Add noodles and cook another 5 minutes or until vegetables are tender.

TIP: For a thicker soup, process the vegetables in a blender or food processor until smooth and return to the soup pot. Add the cooked alphabet noodles and heat.

Per Serving: Calories: 125; % Calories from fat: 4; Fat (gm): 0.6; Saturated fat (gm): 0.1; Cholesterol (mg): 13.2; Sodium (mg): 245; Protein (gm): 6.9; Carbohydrate (gm): 22.8
Exchanges: Milk: 0.0; Vegetable: 2.0; Fruit: 0.0; Bread: 1.0; Meat: 0.0; Fat: 0.0

For extra zip, add 1 can (4 ounces) of drained, chopped mild green chilies. Sprinkle the finished soup with a little reduced-fat shredded Monterey Jack cheese or crumbled goat's cheese.

🔥 **LOW CARB**
🐮 **LOW FAT**

TORTILLA SOUP

MAKES 6 (2-CUP) SERVINGS

1 can (14 1/2 ounces) low-sodium diced tomatoes, including liquid

1 cup chopped green onions

1 tablespoon chopped cilantro

1/2 teaspoon garlic powder

1/8 teaspoon salt

1/8 teaspoon black pepper

1 can (48 ounces) low-sodium chicken broth

Olive oil-flavored nonstick cooking spray

3 whole-wheat 99% fat-free tortillas, cut into strips

Using a food processor or blender, pulse the tomatoes and their liquid with onions and cilantro, garlic powder, salt, and pepper until evenly textured. Pour mixture into a saucepan. Stir in broth.

Bring the soup to a boil over medium heat. Partially cover and simmer for 5 minutes.

While soup cooks, lightly coat a nonstick frying pan with cooking spray. Cook the tortilla strips over medium-high heat, stirring often and spraying once, about 2 minutes or just until crisp.

Ladle the soup into individual bowls and top with tortilla strips.

....

Per Serving: Calories: 88; % Calories from fat: 15; Fat (gm): 1.4; Saturated fat (gm): 0; Cholesterol (mg): 23.6; Sodium (mg): 402; Protein (gm): 8.3; Carbohydrate (gm): 9.6
Exchanges: Milk: 0.0; Vegetable: 0.0; Fruit: 0.0; Bread: 0.5; Meat: 0.0; Fat: 0.5

Matzo balls are dumplings made from finely ground unleavened crackers. Matzo ball mix is available in the specialty foods aisle of most supermarkets. Matzo balls can be made ahead and refrigerated for up to 2 days, or they can be frozen in a single layer on a baking sheet, then placed in resealable plastic freezer bags.

🐄 LOW FAT

CARROT SOUP WITH MATZO BALLS

MAKES 8 (1-CUP) SERVINGS, WITH 1 MATZO BALL PER SERVING

Butter-flavored nonstick cooking spray

1 cup chopped onion

2 cans (14 $\frac{1}{2}$ ounces each) low-sodium vegetable, or chicken, broth

$\frac{1}{8}$ teaspoon salt

$\frac{1}{8}$ teaspoon black pepper

$\frac{1}{4}$ teaspoon ground sage

3 packages (10 ounces each) sliced carrots or 4 cups sliced carrots

3 cups thinly sliced red-skinned potatoes, unpeeled (about 12 ounces)

Matzo Balls (recipe follows)

Lightly coat a nonstick soup pot with cooking spray. Cook the onions over medium heat, stirring occasionally, about 5 minutes.

Stir in the broth, salt, black pepper, sage, carrots, and potatoes. Bring soup to a boil and reduce heat. Simmer for about 15 to 20 minutes, partially covered, until vegetables are tender. Cool slightly.

Process soup in batches in a food processor or blender. Pour the soup back into the soup pot and heat. Ladle soup into bowls and add 1 matzo ball to each bowl.

TIP: Wand or immersion blenders are invaluable for creating smooth soups easily and with less mess. Instead of moving hot soup from a pot to a blender or food processor, a handheld wand blender is immersed into the soup pot. A few pulses, and your soup is smooth and ready to serve, with no lifting, pouring, or ladling into blender jars or processor bowls. Wand blenders are inexpensive and available at kitchen wares stores and most hardware stores.

MATZO BALLS

MAKES 8 BALLS, 1 BALL PER SERVING

$1/2$ cup egg substitute

$1/4$ cup water or reduced-sodium broth

$1/2$ cup matzo meal

2 teaspoons canola-blend oil

$1/8$ teaspoon salt

$1/8$ teaspoon black pepper

Stir together egg substitute, water, matzo meal, oil, salt, and pepper in mixing bowl. Cover and refrigerate for 20 minutes.

Using wet hands, shape dough into 8 balls.

Bring a large pot of lightly salted water to a boil. Slide balls into boiling water. Reduce heat to simmer and cover. Cook 15 minutes. Remove matzo balls with a slotted spoon and drain.

Per Serving: Calories: 122; % Calories from fat: 12; Fat (gm): 1.7; Saturated fat (gm): 0.1; Cholesterol (mg): 0; Sodium (mg): 458; Protein (gm): 4.4; Carbohydrate (gm): 23
Exchanges: Milk: 0.0; Vegetable: 2.0; Fruit: 0.0; Bread: 1.0; Meat: 0.0; Fat: 0.0

Minced garlic and cumin are available in the vegetable section of large supermarkets. Use these products instead of garlic powder and dried cumin for a more intense flavor.

⊛ **LOW FAT**

BLACK BEAN SOUP

MAKES 10 (1-CUP) SERVINGS

    Olive oil-flavored nonstick cooking spray

1 cup chopped onion

1 cup chopped carrot

1 can (28 ounces) low-sodium chicken broth

1 can (14 1/2 ounces) low-sodium diced tomatoes, including liquid

2 cans (15 ounces each) black beans, rinsed, drained, and mashed

1 teaspoon chopped garlic

1/4 teaspoon ground cumin

1/4 teaspoon salt

1/8 teaspoon black pepper

Lightly coat a large soup pot with cooking spray. Cook onion and carrot over medium heat for 5 minutes, stirring occasionally. Stir in broth, tomatoes, beans, garlic, cumin, salt, and pepper. Bring to a boil. Reduce heat to a simmer and cook, partially covered, for about 10 minutes. Cool slightly.

Process soup in batches in a blender or a food processor until smooth. Return soup to pot and heat.

SERVING SUGGESTION: Add ground oregano, ground thyme, and fresh chopped cilantro during cooking for extra flavor. Garnish the soup at the table with chopped white, red, or green onion passed in a small bowl.

•••

Per Serving: Calories: 103; % Calories from fat: 5; Fat (gm): 0.6; Saturated fat (gm): 0; Cholesterol (mg): 8.3; Sodium (mg): 424; Protein (gm): 7; Carbohydrate (gm): 16.2
Exchanges: Milk: 0.0; Vegetable: 0.0; Fruit: 0.0; Bread: 1.0; Meat: 0.5; Fat: 0.0

For a complete meal in a bowl, add bits of leftover meat, chicken, and vegetables to Wonton Soup. Fresh vegetables to add for extra flavor include watercress, snow peas, bamboo shoots, and sliced Chinese cabbage.

◊ LOW CARB
☻ LOW FAT

WONTON SOUP

MAKES 8 (1-CUP) SERVINGS

 1 can (48 ounces) low-sodium chicken broth
 1/4 cup chopped green onions
 Vegetable-Filled Wontons (recipe follows)

Bring broth, onions, and wontons to a boil in a large soup pot. Reduce heat to a simmer and cook for about 5 minutes or until hot.

VEGETABLE-FILLED WONTONS

MAKES 24 WONTONS, OR 8 SERVINGS OF 3

 Butter-flavored nonstick cooking spray
 1/2 cup chopped green onions
 2 cups cleaned, chopped white mushrooms
 Salt and pepper, to taste
 24 wonton wrappers
 1 egg white, lightly beaten

Coat a nonstick frying pan with butter-flavored nonstick cooking spray. Add onions and mushrooms and cook over medium-high heat, stirring occasionally until tender, about 5 minutes. Season with salt and pepper. Cool and drain.

To assemble wontons, place 1 scant tablespoon of filling in the center of each wonton wrapper. Brush edges of wrapper with egg white. Fold wrapper in half, making a triangular shape, and press along edges, sealing wontons. Set wontons on lightly floured nonstick cookie sheet. Cover with plastic wrap to prevent drying.

Fill a medium saucepan half-full of water. Bring to a boil. Slide a batch of the wontons into the water. Cook 1 1/2 to 2 minutes or until wontons are tender. Remove wontons with a slotted spoon and place in a single layer on a sprayed, heated platter. Repeat until all of the wontons are cooked.

Per Serving: Calories: 55; % Calories from fat: 21; Fat (gm): 1.3; Saturated fat (gm): 0; Cholesterol (mg): 18.7; Sodium (mg): 210; Protein (gm): 5.9; Carbohydrate (gm): 4.7
Exchanges: Milk: 0.0; Vegetable: 1.0; Fruit: 0.0; Bread: 0.0; Meat: 0.0; Fat: 0.5

Hot and sour is a popular Chinese soup. For extra flavor, soak dried shiitake mushrooms in hot water until soft enough to slice. Add the sliced mushrooms to the soup, as well as the soaking liquid, discarding any grit left in the bottom of the soaking bowl.

⚬ **LOW CARB**
🐰 **LOW FAT**

EASY HOT AND SOUR SOUP

MAKES 6 (1-CUP) SERVINGS

- 1 can (48 ounces) low-sodium chicken broth
- $3/4$ cup sliced bamboo shoots
- $1/2$ cup chopped green onions
- 1 tablespoon soy sauce
- $1/4$ cup red wine vinegar
- $1/8$ teaspoon black pepper

Bring broth to a boil over medium heat. Add bamboo shoots, onion, soy sauce, vinegar, and pepper. Reduce heat and simmer until hot.

Per Serving: Calories: 52; % Calories from fat: 27; Fat (gm): 1.5; Saturated fat (gm): 0; Cholesterol (mg): 23.6; Sodium (mg): 410; Protein (gm): 7.4; Carbohydrate (gm): 1.9
Exchanges: Milk: 0.0; Vegetable: 1.5; Fruit: 0.0; Bread: 0.0; Meat: 0.0; Fat: 0.5

Cincinnati Chili is a specialty from the city for which it is named. The chili is flavored with cinnamon and served over spaghetti with various condiments. The customers choose their favorite condiments, ordering the dish one way, two way, or three way, depending on the condiments ordered.

CINCINNATI CHILI

MAKES 8 SERVINGS (¾ CUP CHILI, ½ CUP SPAGHETTI PER SERVING)

Olive oil-flavored cooking spray
1 cup chopped onion
1 pound extra-lean ground turkey
1 can (15 ounces) low-sodium kidney beans, rinsed and drained
1 can (14½ ounces) low-sodium crushed tomatoes
1 tablespoon barbecue spice mix
1 teaspoon ground cinnamon
12 ounces uncooked whole-wheat spaghetti

Lightly coat a large nonstick frying pan with cooking spray. Cook the onion and turkey over medium heat, stirring occasionally, for 5 to 6 minutes or until onion is soft and the turkey is no longer pink.

Add the beans, tomatoes, spice mix, and cinnamon. Cook about 4 minutes, crushing some of the beans with the back of a spoon, or until hot.

While the chili cooks, prepare the spaghetti according to package directions, omitting salt. Drain.

To serve, divide the hot spaghetti among servings bowls. Ladle the chili over the pasta.

SERVING SUGGESTION: Traditional toppers for Cincinnati Chili include oyster crackers, grated Cheddar cheese, chopped tomatoes, and minced onion. If using cheese, choose a low-fat variety and use a small amount, about 1 tablespoon per serving.

This is a good, basic chili recipe to have on hand. For variety, serve it over whole-wheat elbow macaroni for a quick chili mac dish.

☙ LOW FAT

15-MINUTE CHILI

MAKES 8 (1-CUP) SERVINGS

Olive oil-flavored nonstick cooking spray
4 ounces 90% lean ground beef
1 cup chopped onion
1 cup chopped celery
1 cup chopped green bell pepper
1 can (14 ½ ounces) low-sodium chopped tomatoes, including liquid
2 cans (16 ounces each) kidney beans, drained and rinsed
1 teaspoon barbecue spice mix

Lightly coat a nonstick frying pan with cooking spray. Cook the beef and onion, stirring occasionally and breaking up the meat, until the onion is tender and the meat is no longer pink, about 3 minutes. Add the celery and bell pepper. Cover and cook 4 to 5 minutes or until the vegetables are tender.

Stir in the tomatoes and their liquid, beans, and spice mix. Add water by the ¼ cup if the mixture is too dry. Cover and simmer for 10 minutes or until hot.

....

Per Serving: Calories: 144; % Calories from fat: 8; Fat (gm): 1.3; Saturated fat (gm): 0.3; Cholesterol (mg): 8.3; Sodium (mg): 421; Protein (gm): 10; Carbohydrate (gm): 23.1
Exchanges: Milk: 0.0; Vegetable: 1.0; Fruit: 0.0; Bread: 1.0; Meat: 1.0; Fat: 0.0

CHAPTER FIVE

Main Dishes

These easy turnovers can also be prepared in the microwave and on indoor electric grills.

TORTILLA TURNOVERS

MAKES 4 SERVINGS, 1 TURNOVER PER SERVING

4 flour tortillas, preferably whole-wheat

1 cup cooked ground chicken, lean beef, or turkey

$1/2$ cup (2 ounces) shredded reduced-fat Monterey Jack, or Cheddar, cheese

$1/2$ cup bottled, or homemade, salsa (recipe on Page 109)

Olive oil-flavored nonstick cooking spray

Lay tortillas on counter and spread meat on half of each tortilla. Sprinkle 1 tablespoon cheese and 1 tablespoon salsa over the meat. Fold tortillas in half.

Lightly coat a large nonstick skillet with cooking spray. Cook turnovers over medium heat, covered, turning once, until lightly browned on both sides and heated through, about 5 minutes.

Per Serving: Calories: 201; % Calories from fat: 29; Fat (gm): 6.4; Saturated fat (gm): 2.9; Cholesterol (mg): 36.9; Sodium (mg): 364; Protein (gm): 16.6; Carbohydrate (gm): 19
Exchanges: Milk: 0.0; Vegetable: 0.0; Fruit: 0.0; Bread: 1.0; Meat: 2.0; Fat: 0.0

Here's a dressed up version of macaroni and cheese that is fare fit for company.

🐄 LOW FAT

COMPANY MACARONI AND CHEESE

MAKES 8 (1-CUP) SERVINGS

  3 cups uncooked macaroni (12 ounces)
  2 tablespoons reduced-fat margarine
  1/2 cup minced onion
  1/4 cup all-purpose flour
  2 cups skim milk
  3/4 cup reduced-fat mozzarella, or Cheddar, cheese
  1 cup chopped green pepper
  1 teaspoon prepared mustard
  2 tablespoons unflavored breadcrumbs

Preheat oven to 350 degrees F.

Cook macaroni according to package directions, omitting salt. Drain and set aside.

Heat margarine in fry pan over medium heat. Cook onions in margarine for a few minutes or until translucent, stirring occasionally. Whisk in flour. Pour in 1/2 cup of the milk and continue whisking until smooth. Add remaining milk and cook a few minutes, whisking until sauce thickens slightly. Remove from heat and whisk in cheese, green pepper, and mustard.

Put drained macaroni in a 2-quart casserole. Stir in cheese sauce. Sprinkle with breadcrumbs. Bake for 20 minutes or until hot.

Per Serving: Calories: 245; % Calories from fat: 13; Fat (gm): 3.8; Saturated fat (gm): 1.3; Cholesterol (mg): 5.4; Sodium (mg): 149; Protein (gm): 11; Carbohydrate (gm): 41.3
Exchanges: Milk: 0.0; Vegetable: 0.0; Fruit: 0.0; Bread: 3.0; Meat: 0.0; Fat: 0.5

Egg foo yong is an Asian omelet with vegetables. For extra flavor add $1/2$ cup sliced mushrooms along with the green onions and sprouts or substitute shredded carrots for the bean sprouts.

◔ **LOW CARB**
🐮 **LOW FAT**

EGG FOO YONG

MAKES 8 PANCAKES, OR 4 SERVINGS OF 2 PANCAKES

SAUCE:

- 1 cup low-sodium vegetable broth
- 1 tablespoon cornstarch
- 2 teaspoons light soy sauce

PANCAKES:

- 1 $1/2$ cups egg substitute, or 6 eggs
- $1/8$ teaspoon salt
- $1/8$ teaspoon black pepper
- $1/8$ teaspoon garlic powder
- Nonstick cooking spray
- $3/4$ cup minced green onions
- $3/4$ cup bean sprouts

Heat the broth in a small saucepan over medium heat. Remove $1/4$ cup of the broth and whisk together with the cornstarch in a small bowl. Return the cornstarch mixture to saucepan and whisk in. Whisk in soy sauce. Continue cooking until sauce thickens slightly, about 1 minute. Set aside.

To make pancakes, pour the egg substitute into a large mixing bowl. Stir in the salt, black pepper, and garlic powder. Set aside

Lightly coat a nonstick frying pan with cooking spray. Heat over medium heat. Add onions and cook for about 1 minute. Add bean sprouts and cook 1 minute, stirring occasionally. Remove pan from heat. Remove vegetables and add to mixing bowl with egg substitute and seasonings.

Wipe pan clean with paper towel and lightly coat with spray. Heat over medium heat. Spoon 2 to 3 tablespoons of vegetable/egg batter into pan for each pancake. Cook until firm and lightly browned, turning once, about 2 minutes for each side. Drizzle pancakes with sauce before serving.

Per Serving: Calories: 75; % Calories from fat: 2; Fat (gm): 0.2; Saturated fat (gm): 0; Cholesterol (mg): 0; Sodium (mg): 449; Protein (gm): 10.5; Carbohydrate (gm): 7.6
Exchanges: Milk: 0.0; Vegetable: 0.0; Fruit: 0.0; Bread: 0.0; Meat: 1.5; Fat: 0.0

White or yellow corn tortillas can be substituted for flour tortillas.

SOFT TACOS

MAKES 6 SERVINGS

6 flour tortillas (6 inches in diameter)

Olive oil-flavored nonstick cooking spray

$1/4$ cup chopped onion

1 teaspoon chili powder or more to taste

6 ounces lean ground beef (85 % lean)

$1 \, 1/2$ cups chopped romaine lettuce

$3/4$ chopped tomato

4 ounces reduced-fat Cheddar cheese

$3/4$ cup fat-free plain yogurt

Preheat oven to 325 degrees F. Sprinkle each tortilla lightly with water. Wrap tortillas in aluminum foil and place in the oven.

Heat a nonstick frying pan coated with olive oil-flavored nonstick cooking spray over medium heat. Add the onion and season with chili powder. Mix in the meat and cook until no longer pink. Drain off any fat.

Remove tortillas from the oven and lay out on a work surface. Divide the beef equally among the tortillas. Top with lettuce, tomato, cheese, and yogurt. Fold tortillas in half.

Per Serving: Calories: 254; % Calories from fat: 39; Fat (gm): 10.9; Saturated fat (gm): 5; Cholesterol (mg): 33; Sodium (mg): 363; Protein (gm): 15.1; Carbohydrate (gm): 22.7
Exchanges: Milk: 0.0; Vegetable: 0.0; Fruit: 0.0; Bread: 1.5; Meat: 1.5; Fat: 1.5

Many children love to help prepare food, so let them in on the fun. Young children can help assemble the burritos; older ones can help with the cooking and chopping.

🐮 LOW FAT

BEAN BURRITOS

MAKES 4 BURRITOS, 1 BURRITO PER SERVING

Olive oil-flavored cooking spray
1 can (16 ounces) fat-free, reduced-sodium refried beans
1 teaspoon chili powder
4 (6-inch) flour tortillas
4 tablespoons grated low-fat Monterey Jack cheese
2 cups chopped lettuce

Heat a large nonstick frying pan lightly coated with cooking spray over medium heat Add the beans and stir in the chili powder. Continue heating until the beans are smooth and heated. Remove from heat.

Spoon beans over the tortillas. Sprinkle with cheese and lettuce.

Roll burritos up.

SERVING SUGGESTION: Drizzle salsa of your choice over filling and add sliced avocado.

Per Serving: Calories: 204; % Calories from fat: 17; Fat (gm): 4.3; Saturated fat (gm): 1.6; Cholesterol (mg): 5; Sodium (mg): 673; Protein (gm): 10.7; Carbohydrate (gm): 36.1
Exchanges: Milk: 0.0; Vegetable: 0.0; Fruit: 0.0; Bread: 2.5; Meat: 0.0; Fat: 0.5

For an authentic taste treat, serve these Thai-Style Noodles with Thai Peanut Sauce (recipe on Page 115).

🐮 LOW FAT
◇ LOW SODIUM

THAI-STYLE NOODLES

MAKES 6 (1-CUP) SERVINGS

6 ounces uncooked whole-wheat spaghetti
1 cup chopped peeled cucumber
1 cup grated carrots
1 cup bean sprouts
1/2 cup chopped cilantro

Cook spaghetti according to package directions, omitting salt. Drain.

Divide pasta among 6 bowls. Top with cucumber, carrot, and bean sprouts. Sprinkle cilantro over vegetables.

Per Serving: Calories: 115; % Calories from fat: 4; Fat (gm): 0.5; Saturated fat (gm): 0.1; Cholesterol (mg): 0; Sodium (mg): 9; Protein (gm): 5; Carbohydrate (gm): 24.8
Exchanges: Milk: 0.0; Vegetable: 0.0; Fruit: 0.0; Bread: 1.5; Meat: 0.0; Fat: 0.0

CHAPTER SIX

Beef Dishes

Every busy household should have a slow cooker, which is great for cooking stews like this one. If using a slow cooker, brown the meat on the stovetop then transfer to the slow cooker with the vegetables, half the liquids, and the seasonings. Cook the stew for about 6 hours on LOW.

COMFORT BEEF STEW

MAKES 8 SERVINGS

- 1 pound boneless, lean beef chuck, cut into 1- or 2-inch chunks
- 2 packages (2 pounds each) frozen mixed stew vegetables
- 1 can (8 ounces) low-sodium tomato sauce
- 1 cup fat-free, low-sodium beef broth
- 1/4 teaspoon salt
- 1/4 teaspoon black pepper
- 1/2 teaspoon chopped garlic

Brown the meat in a heavy-bottomed stewpot or high-sided frying pan with lid over medium-high heat, turning meat several times to brown on all sides. Add vegetables, tomato sauce, broth, salt, black pepper, and chopped garlic.

Simmer the stew partially covered for 1 hour, stirring occasionally. Remove lid and continue cooking until beef is tender, about 30 minutes.

....

Per Serving: Calories: 226; % Calories from fat: 32; Fat (gm): 8.1; Saturated fat (gm): 3.2; Cholesterol (mg): 37.1; Sodium (mg): 238; Protein (gm): 14.3; Carbohydrate (gm): 23.7
Exchanges: Milk: 0.0; Vegetable: 2.0; Fruit: 0.0; Bread: 1.0; Meat: 1.0; Fat: 1.0

Use your standard-sized muffin pan to make these fun individual-sized meatloaves. For special occasions, "frost" the muffins with hot mashed potatoes.

◔ LOW CARB
◇ LOW SODIUM

MEATLOAF MUFFINS

MAKES 12 MEATLOAVES, 1 PER SERVING

1 ¼ pounds lean (90%) ground beef
½ cup whole-wheat bread crumbs (see note)
¼ cup egg substitute
½ cup chopped onion
1 cup chopped celery
½ teaspoon Italian seasoning mix
  Canola oil-flavored nonstick cooking spray

Position oven rack in center of oven and preheat oven to 375 degrees F. Mix together beef, bread crumbs, egg substitute, onions, celery, and seasoning mix in large bowl.

Lightly coat 2 (6-cup) or 1 (12-cup) nonstick muffin pans with cooking spray. Mound meat mixture into muffin cups. Bake about 30 minutes or until meatloaves are browned and juices run clear.

NOTE: To make bread crumbs, process torn slices of stale bread in a food processor or blender for 30 to 45 seconds or until crumbs are formed.

VARIATION: Use a blend of beef and pork.

Per Serving: Calories: 106; % Calories from fat: 41; Fat (gm): 4.7; Saturated fat (gm): 1.7; Cholesterol (mg): 28.8; Sodium (mg): 85; Protein (gm): 11; Carbohydrate (gm): 4.3
Exchanges: Milk: 0.0; Vegetable: 0.0; Fruit: 0.0; Bread: 0.0; Meat: 2.0; Fat: 0.0

For easier slicing, use a Japanese trick and chill the meat in the freezer, nearly to the point of freezing, and always cut against the grain.

⦿ **LOW CARB**

GRILLED FLANK STEAK ON SALAD GREENS

MAKES 8 SERVINGS OF 2 OUNCES MEAT AND 1½ CUPS VEGETABLES

- 8 cups assorted greens or spinach, washed and drained
  Olive oil-flavored nonstick cooking spray
- 1 bunch fresh asparagus, bottom ends trimmed
- 2 cups sliced tomatoes
- ¾ cup calorie-free balsamic vinaigrette
- 1 pound lean flank steak, sliced

Arrange the greens on 8 dinner plates.

Lightly coat a nonstick, indoor electric or stovetop grill or nonstick fry pan with cooking spray and preheat. Grill or pan fry the asparagus over medium heat, about 4 minutes or until slightly browned and tender-crisp. Cut asparagus in 2-inch pieces and scatter over the greens. Arrange tomatoes over the asparagus. Drizzle ½ cup dressing equally over salads.

Brush the steak slices with the remaining ¼ cup vinaigrette. Grill or pan fry the steak 5 to 7 minutes or until desired doneness. Arrange the steak over the salads.

VARIATION: For a Russian or Middle Eastern flavor, substitute lean leg of lamb for the beef.

....

Per Serving: Calories: 119; % Calories from fat: 31; Fat (gm): 4.1; Saturated fat (gm): 1.7; Cholesterol (mg): 22.8; Sodium (mg): 330; Protein (gm): 14.6; Carbohydrate (gm): 6.3
Exchanges: Milk: 0.0; Vegetable: 1.0; Fruit: 0.0; Bread: 0.0; Meat: 2.0; Fat: 0.0

To prevent charring, soak bamboo or wooden skewers in water for 20 minutes before threading on the meat and vegetables.

⚱ LOW CARB
🐄 LOW FAT
◇ LOW SODIUM

SHISH KABOBS

MAKES 4 SKEWERS, 1 SKEWER PER SERVING

    4 ounces sirloin steak, trimmed of fat and cubed
    1 cup fat-free Russian salad dressing
   16 cherry tomatoes
    2 cups square-cut seeded red bell pepper
   16 mushrooms, cleaned and stems removed
    4 wooden, or metal, skewers

Toss steak with dressing in a glass bowl. Cover lightly with plastic wrap and refrigerate overnight, turning steak once or twice.

Just before cooking, remove steak from marinade. Discard marinade.

Thread skewers with meat, tomatoes, peppers, and mushrooms.

Preheat the outdoor grill, stovetop or electric indoor grill, or broiler. Cook skewers, turning every 4 minutes, until beef is cooked to desired doneness.

SERVING SUGGESTION: Serve kabobs wrapped in whole-wheat pita pockets or with whole-grain couscous, if your eating plan allows.

Per Serving: Calories: 99; % Calories from fat: 16; Fat (gm): 1.9; Saturated fat (gm): 0.5; Cholesterol (mg): 17.2; Sodium (mg): 84; Protein (gm): 9.4; Carbohydrate (gm): 13.1
Exchanges: Milk: 0.0; Vegetable: 2.0; Fruit: 0.0; Bread: 0.0; Meat: 1.0; Fat: 0.0

Serve Beef Satay with sliced cucumbers sprinkled with chopped green onions. For extra zip, sprinkle a little mild curry powder on the beef before grilling.

⚙ **LOW CARB**
◇ **LOW SODIUM**

BEEF SATAY

MAKES 8 SKEWERS, 1 SKEWER PER SERVING

> 1 pound flank steak or sirloin, cut in thin slices against the grain
>
> $1/2$ cup fat-free red wine salad dressing
>
> 6 bamboo skewers, soaked in water 20 minutes

Thread beef strips onto skewers. Place skewers in a glass dish and brush with dressing. Let meat marinate for 2 hours. Remove from marinade and drain. Discard marinade.

Preheat stovetop or electric indoor grill according to manufacturer's instructions, or use broiler. Grill meat a few minutes on each side to desired doneness.

SERVING SUGGESTION: Serve, if desired, with Thai Peanut Sauce (recipe on Page 115).

Per Serving: Calories: 89; % Calories from fat: 41; Fat (gm): 3.9; Saturated fat (gm): 1.7; Cholesterol (mg): 22.8; Sodium (mg): 50; Protein (gm): 12.4; Carbohydrate (gm): 0.1
Exchanges: Milk: 0.0; Vegetable: 0.0; Fruit: 0.0; Bread: 0.0; Meat: 1.5; Fat: 0.0

CHAPTER SEVEN

Turkey and Chicken

Kids love mini-sized Turkey Muffins, which are simply kid-sized versions of meatloaf. For an adult-sized portion, use a 6-count muffin pan. Serve Turkey Muffins with Marinara Sauce (recipe on Page 113).

◔ **LOW CARB**
◇ **LOW SODIUM**

TURKEY MUFFINS

MAKES 12 MINI MUFFINS OR 6 MAIN-DISH MUFFINS
(NUTRITIONAL ANALYSIS BASED ON 1 MINI MUFFIN)

Olive oil-flavored nonstick cooking spray

1 pound lean ground turkey

1/4 cup Barbecue Sauce (recipe on Page 111) or store-bought or ketchup, preferably reduced sugar and reduced sodium

3/4 cup soft white bread crumbs (see note)

1/2 cup chopped onion

1/4 cup egg substitute

1 teaspoon Worcestershire sauce

1 teaspoon garlic powder

1 teaspoon prepared mustard

Position rack in center of oven and preheat oven to 350 degrees F. Lightly spray a 12-count mini muffin pan or a 6-count regular muffin pan with cooking spray.

Combine turkey with Barbecue Sauce, bread crumbs, onion, egg substitute, Worcestershire sauce, garlic powder, and mustard in large mixing bowl.

Divide mixture into 12 mini or 6 adult portions. Shape into balls and place in muffin pan.

Bake for about 25 minutes for mini and about 30 minutes for larger muffins or until juices run clear.

NOTE: To make bread crumbs, process torn slices of stale bread in a food processor or blender for 30 to 45 seconds or until crumbs are formed.

Per Serving: Calories: 75; % Calories from fat: 42; Fat (gm): 3.4; Saturated fat (gm): 0.9; Cholesterol (mg): 29.9; Sodium (mg): 100; Protein (gm): 7.6; Carbohydrate (gm): 3
Exchanges: Milk: 0.0; Vegetable: 0.0; Fruit: 0.0; Bread: 0.0; Meat: 1.0; Fat: 0.5

For the bean and legume family, lentils are high in fiber but relatively low in carbohydrate, making it an excellent food choice for healthy eating. Lentils also cook much more quickly than beans and do not need presoaking.

◇ LOW SODIUM

TURKEY AND LENTILS

MAKES 6 (1-CUP) SERVINGS

- 1 cup uncooked green lentils
- 2 cups reduced-sodium chicken broth
- 1 bay leaf
- 5 ounces skinless, roasted, cubed turkey, breast meat only
- 2 cups bean sprouts, washed and drained
- 1/2 cup fresh mint leaves
- 1/4 cup oil and vinegar salad dressing

Bring to a boil the lentils, chicken broth, and bay leaf in a saucepan. Reduce the heat to a simmer. Cook for 25 minutes or until the lentils are tender. Drain the lentils and rinse, discarding the bay leaf.

Toss the lentils with the turkey, bean sprouts, mint leaves, and salad dressing in a large salad bowl.

Cover lightly and refrigerate until ready to serve. Serve chilled or at room temperature.

Per Serving: Calories: 214; % Calories from fat: 26; Fat (gm): 6.3; Saturated fat (gm): 1.1; Cholesterol (mg): 27.9; Sodium (mg): 102; Protein (gm): 19.5; Carbohydrate (gm): 20.9
Exchanges: Milk: 0.0; Vegetable: 1.0; Fruit: 0.0; Bread: 1.0; Meat: 2.0; Fat: 0.0

For a delicious dinner, serve BBQ Chicken Breast with Coleslaw (recipe on Page 32) and Buttermilk Corn Muffins (recipe on Page 119).

🔥 **LOW CARB**
🐄 **LOW FAT**

BBQ CHICKEN BREAST

MAKES 6 SERVINGS, ABOUT 3 OUNCES CHICKEN PER SERVING

Butter-flavored nonstick cooking spray
1 pound skinless, boneless chicken breast halves (about 4)
$1/2$ cup Barbecue Sauce (recipe on Page 111) or store-bought

Position rack in center of oven and preheat oven to 425 degrees F. Lightly coat a shallow baking pan with butter-flavored cooking spray.

Place chicken in the pan and brush with half of the sauce. Cover the pan with aluminum foil and bake for 35 minutes.

Uncover and bake 10 minutes or until the chicken is no longer pink in the center. Brush with remaining sauce. Remove from oven and slice into 6 portions.

Per Serving: Calories: 98; % Calories from fat: 12; Fat (gm): 1.3; Saturated fat (gm): 0.3; Cholesterol (mg): 43.8; Sodium (mg): 209; Protein (gm): 17.8; Carbohydrate (gm): 2.7
Exchanges: Milk: 0.0; Vegetable: 0.0; Fruit: 0.0; Bread: 0.0; Meat: 2.0; Fat: 0.0

To speed preparation, keep on hand in the refrigerator bottles of store-bought minced garlic and minced ginger. Or mince your own and keep in the freezer in small, resealable plastic food storage bags.

⏻ **LOW CARB**
🐮 **LOW FAT**
◇ **LOW SODIUM**

MOO GOO GAI PAN

MAKES 8 (½-CUP) SERVINGS

    Vegetable oil-flavored nonstick cooking spray
½ teaspoon minced ginger
½ teaspoon minced garlic
½ pound skinless, boneless chicken breast halves (about 2), cubed
1¼ cups reduced-sodium chicken broth
2 cups chopped tomatoes
2 cups shredded cabbage
2 tablespoons cornstarch

Lightly coat a nonstick frying pan with cooking spray. Cook ginger, garlic, and chicken over medium-high heat, stirring constantly and spraying once. Cook, stirring, until the chicken is almost cooked through, about 3 minutes.

Add ¾ cup broth to the pan. Stir in tomatoes and cabbage.

Whisk together cornstarch and remaining ½ cup broth in small bowl. Stir cornstarch mixture into pan and continue cooking until sauce thickens slightly and chicken is no longer pink.

Per Serving: Calories: 60; % Calories from fat: 11; Fat (gm): 0.8; Saturated fat (gm): 0.1; Cholesterol (mg): 20.3; Sodium (mg): 61; Protein (gm): 8.3; Carbohydrate (gm): 4.9
Exchanges: Milk: 0.0; Vegetable: 1.0; Fruit: 0.0; Bread: 0.0; Meat: 0.5; Fat: 0.0

With a couple of stir-fry dishes in your cooking repertoire, you'll always be able to make a delicious meal in no time.

◌ LOW CARB
♨ LOW FAT
◇ LOW SODIUM

CHICKEN MUSHROOM STIR-FRY

MAKES 6 (1-CUP) SERVINGS

Oil-flavored nonstick cooking spray
1 cup chopped green onions
1 teaspoon chopped garlic
1 teaspoon chopped ginger
3/4 cup shredded cooked skinless chicken
2 cups diagonally sliced celery
3 cups sliced mushrooms
3/4 cup reduced-sodium chicken broth
2 tablespoons cornstarch

Lightly coat a nonstick frying pan or wok with cooking spray. Cook the onion, garlic, and ginger over medium heat, stirring constantly, for 1 minute.

Stir in the chicken, celery, and mushrooms. Cook a few minutes, stirring constantly, until vegetables are tender-crisp.

Whisk together the broth and cornstarch in a small bowl. Stir the mixture into the chicken and vegetables. Cook until the sauce thickens slightly, about 1 minute.

Per Serving: Calories: 68; % Calories from fat: 20; Fat (gm): 1.6; Saturated fat (gm): 0.4; Cholesterol (mg): 17.6; Sodium (mg): 83; Protein (gm): 7.3; Carbohydrate (gm): 6.8
Exchanges: Milk: 0.0; Vegetable: 1.0; Fruit: 0.0; Bread: 0.0; Meat: 1.0; Fat: 0.0

Canola oil is lower in saturated fat than any other oil, and it contains more cholesterol-balancing monounsaturated fat than any oil except olive oil. Canola also contains omega-3 fatty acids, a beneficial fat thought to lower the "bad" cholesterol. The mild-flavored oil can be used for cooking and salad dressings.

⟡ **LOW CARB**

STIR-FRIED CHICKEN WITH PEANUTS

MAKES 6 (³⁄₄-CUP) SERVINGS

- 2 tablespoons canola-blend oil
- 2 ounces skinless, boneless chicken breast, cubed (about 1 cup)
- 2 cups snow peas, ends trimmed
- 1 cup sliced, drained bamboo shoots
- ¼ cup unsalted peanuts
- 3 tablespoons store-bought stir-fry sauce

Heat the oil in a nonstick frying pan or wok over medium-high heat. Add the chicken and cook, stirring often, about 4 minutes or until the chicken is cooked through. If the chicken becomes dry, add a little water or low-sodium chicken broth.

Stir in the snow peas, bamboo shoots, peanuts, and sauce. Cook, stirring, until peas are tender-crisp and hot, about 2 minutes.

Per Serving: Calories: 109; % Calories from fat: 63; Fat (gm): 7.8; Saturated fat (gm): 0.8; Cholesterol (mg): 5.5; Sodium (mg): 268; Protein (gm): 4.8; Carbohydrate (gm): 5.6
Exchanges: Milk: 0.0; Vegetable: 1.0; Fruit: 0.0; Bread: 0.0; Meat: 1.0; Fat: 1.0

This is great for a children's party. Use small drumsticks to maintain portion control.

⏚ LOW CARB
🐮 LOW FAT
◇ LOW SODIUM

OVEN-FRIED CHICKEN DRUMSTICKS

MAKES 8 SERVINGS, 1 DRUMSTICK PER SERVING

Butter-flavored cooking spray
8 small chicken drumsticks, skin removed
1 cup crushed whole-grain cereal
$1/3$ cup egg substitute

Place oven rack in center of oven and preheat oven to 400 degrees F. Lightly coat a baking sheet with cooking spray.

Rinse chicken and pat dry with paper towels. Put cereal on a piece of waxed paper and the egg substitute in a shallow bowl. Roll each drumstick in egg substitute and then in crumbs. Press crumbs into drumsticks.

Place drumsticks on baking sheet. Bake for 45 minutes or until chicken is no longer pink and juices run clear. Let chicken cool for 5 minutes before serving.

Per Serving: Calories: 118; % Calories from fat: 18; Fat (gm): 2.3; Saturated fat (gm): 0.5; Cholesterol (mg): 43.6; Sodium (mg): 138; Protein (gm): 13.5; Carbohydrate (gm): 9.7
Exchanges: Milk: 0.0; Vegetable: 0.0; Fruit: 0.0; Bread: 0.5; Meat: 1.5; Fat: 0.0

Serve Chicken Fingers with salsa or barbecue sauce or, better yet, a mixture of each.

☙ LOW FAT

CHICKEN FINGERS

MAKES 6 SERVINGS, 2 OUNCES PER SERVING

Butter-flavored nonstick cooking spray

3/4 pound skinless, boneless chicken breast meat, cut into fingers

1 cup crushed whole-grain cereal

1/4 cup dry bread crumbs

1/4 cup fat-free ranch-style dressing

Place rack in center of oven and preheat oven to 400 degrees F. Spray a baking sheet with cooking spray.

Combine the cereal crumbs and bread crumbs on waxed paper. Pour the dressing into a shallow bowl. Dip each chicken strip into the dressing and roll in the crumbs.

Place chicken fingers on baking sheet. Bake for 18 to 20 minutes or until chicken is no longer pink in the center.

....

Per Serving: Calories: 158; % Calories from fat: 9; Fat (gm): 1.5; Saturated fat (gm): 0.2; Cholesterol (mg): 32.9; Sodium (mg): 290; Protein (gm): 14.8; Carbohydrate (gm): 19.7
Exchanges: Milk: 0.0; Vegetable: 0.0; Fruit: 0.0; Bread: 1.0; Meat: 2.0; Fat: 0.0

This is a great dish for "planned overs." With already-cooked potatoes and chicken, the dish comes together in a snap. Or you can purchase frozen potato wedges and roasted chicken from the supermarket. Bagged, pre-washed spinach is another time-saver.

🐮 LOW FAT

CHICKEN AND RED POTATOES SALAD

MAKES 6 (2-CUP) SERVINGS

1 ¼ pounds red potatoes, cooked and quartered
³⁄₄ cup chopped roasted chicken, white meat only
4 cups prewashed baby spinach
1 cup sliced red bell pepper
¹⁄₄ cup chopped cilantro
¹⁄₄ cup sliced red onion
¹⁄₄ cup fat-free ranch dressing

Using a large salad bowl, toss together the potatoes, chicken, spinach, red bell pepper, cilantro, and onion. Toss mixture with dressing.

Cover lightly and refrigerate until ready to serve. Spoon salad onto individual salad plates and serve.

Per Serving: Calories: 128; % Calories from fat: 10; Fat (gm): 1.4; Saturated fat (gm): 0.4; Cholesterol (mg): 15.6; Sodium (mg): 191; Protein (gm): 7.1; Carbohydrate (gm): 22.5
Exchanges: Milk: 0.0; Vegetable: 0.0; Fruit: 0.0; Bread: 1.5; Meat: 0.5; Fat: 0.0

Kasha is made from toasted buckwheat groats and has a toasty, nutty flavor. It is cooked like rice, in boiling water that is reduced to a simmer until all of the liquid is absorbed. Kasha is available in most supermarkets, in the kosher or international foods aisle, or in natural foods markets.

♂ **LOW CARB**
🐮 **LOW FAT**
◈ **LOW SODIUM**

CHICKEN KASHA SALAD

MAKES 9 SERVINGS

> 2 cups cooked kasha
> 3/4 cup shredded cooked skinless chicken
> 2 cups sliced cucumber
> 1/2 cup chopped parsley
> 2 tablespoons fat-free French-style salad dressing

Toss together the kasha, chicken, cucumbers, parsley, and dressing in a large salad bowl.

Cover and refrigerate until ready to serve. To serve, place in bowls or on lettuce-garnished serving plates. Serve chilled or at room temperature.

Per Serving: Calories: 64; % Calories from fat: 14; Fat (gm): 1; Saturated fat (gm): 0.3; Cholesterol (mg): 9.7; Sodium (mg): 45; Protein (gm): 4.7; Carbohydrate (gm): 9.5
Exchanges: Milk: 0.0; Vegetable: 0.0; Fruit: 0.0; Bread: 1.0; Meat: 0.0; Fat: 0.0

CHAPTER EIGHT

Seafood

This is an easy dish to make for a last-minute dinner. If you wish, substitute peeled shrimp for the scallops, or use a mixture.

👌 **LOW CARB**
🐮 **LOW FAT**

SCALLOPS WITH ASPARAGUS

MAKES 4 (1½-CUP) SERVINGS

Canola oil-flavored nonstick cooking spray
½ cup chopped green onion
1 pound asparagus, stems trimmed, cut into 1½ inch pieces
¾ pound small scallops
¼ cup store-bought stir-fry sauce

Lightly coat a large nonstick frying pan or wok with cooking spray. Cook the green onions and asparagus, stirring constantly, about 2 minutes.

Add the scallops and sauce. Continue cooking and stirring until the scallops are opaque and firm to the touch, about 2 minutes.

NOTE: Stir-fry sauce is available in the Asian section of most supermarkets and in specialty markets.

....

Per Serving: Calories: 125; % Calories from fat: 6; Fat (gm): 0.9; Saturated fat (gm): 0.1; Cholesterol (mg): 28.1; Sodium (mg): 661; Protein (gm): 17.6; Carbohydrate (gm): 12.1
Exchanges: Milk: 0.0; Vegetable: 2.0; Fruit: 0.0; Bread: 0.0; Meat: 2.0; Fat: 0.0

There are hundreds of varieties of Chinese or Asian noodles, and your supermarket specialty or Asian foods aisle is likely to have a couple of them. For this dish, wheat-based noodles work well. For a change of pace, experiment with rice-based Asian noodles.

🐮 LOW FAT

SHRIMP WITH NOODLES

MAKES 8 (1-CUP) SERVINGS

> 9 ounces wheat-based dry Chinese noodles or thin egg noodles
>
> Canola oil-flavored nonstick cooking spray
>
> 1/2 cup chopped green onions
>
> 1/2 teaspoon minced gingerroot or powdered ginger
>
> 1/4 teaspoon salt
>
> 1/4 teaspoon black pepper
>
> 1/2 pound extra-large shrimp, peeled and deveined
>
> 3 cups fresh bean sprouts, rinsed and drained
>
> 3 tablespoons stir-fry sauce

Cook the noodles according to package directions, omitting salt. Drain and cool.

Lightly coat a large nonstick frying pan with cooking spray. Spread the noodles evenly over the bottom of the pan, forming a single large pancake shape. Fry the noodle cake over medium-high heat until lightly browned on the bottom, about 3 minutes.

Turn the noodle cake over using a large spatula, or slide it out onto a dinner plate and flip back into pan, uncooked side down. Cook until golden, about 3 minutes. Slide noodle cake onto a serving dish and keep warm.

Lightly coat the frying pan with cooking spray. Cook the green onions with gingerroot, salt, and black pepper, stirring constantly, until hot and tender-crisp, about 1 minute. Add the shrimp and bean spouts. Cook, stirring constantly, until the shrimp are opaque and firm to the touch.

Stir in the sauce and heat. Ladle shrimp mixture over noodles.

Per Serving: Calories: 164; % Calories from fat: 5; Fat (gm): 0.9; Saturated fat (gm): 0.3; Cholesterol (mg): 43.1; Sodium (mg): 386; Protein (gm): 7.3; Carbohydrate (gm): 31.7
Exchanges: Milk: 0.0; Vegetable: 0.0; Fruit: 0.0; Bread: 2.0; Meat: 1.0; Fat: 0.0

Cold-water fish such as salmon contain heart-protective omega-3 fatty acids. Most Americans consume far too many omega-6 fatty acids found in red meat and not nearly enough omega-3s.

⭘ **LOW CARB**

ROASTED SALMON

MAKES 5 SERVINGS, 3 OUNCES SALMON PER SERVING

   Butter-flavored nonstick cooking spray

1 cup fat-free mayonnaise

1 tablespoon dry mustard

2 teaspoons dill

1 large (1 pound) skinless salmon fillet, cut into 5 pieces

Position rack in center of oven and preheat the oven to 350 degrees F. Lightly coat a nonstick baking sheet with cooking spray. Mix the mayonnaise, mustard, and dill in a bowl. Put the salmon on the baking sheet and brush with the mayonnaise mixture.

Bake for 20 minutes or until the salmon is opaque, firm to the touch, and flakes easily.

SERVING SUGGESTION: Serve with a leafy green salad and fat-free vinaigrette salad dressing.

....

Per Serving: Calories: 187; % Calories from fat: 50; Fat (gm): 9.9; Saturated fat (gm): 2.3; Cholesterol (mg): 59.4; Sodium (mg): 235; Protein (gm): 18.8; Carbohydrate (gm): 3.7
Exchanges: Milk: 0.0; Vegetable: 0.0; Fruit: 0.0; Bread: 0.0; Meat: 2.5; Fat: 1.0

Use any firm-textured, mild-flavored white fish, such as cat-fish, tilapia, or haddock. Vary the fish and vegetables as you wish, for instance, salmon with sliced red potatoes and green onions. These packages are great to assemble ahead of time and freeze. Thaw the frozen packets before baking.

◔ **LOW CARB**
◇ **LOW SODIUM**

FISH IN A PACKET

MAKES 4 PACKETS, 1 PACKET PER SERVING

    Butter-flavored nonstick cooking spray
- 4 skinless white fish fillets (4 ounces each)
- 4 sheets of aluminum foil or parchment baking paper, cut into 10-inch squares
- 2 cups sliced mushrooms
- 1/2 cup sliced zucchini
- 2 teaspoons Italian seasoning mix

Preheat the oven to 350 degrees F. Spray a baking sheet. Place 1 fillet in the center of each sprayed foil square. Arrange the vegetables over the fish. Sprinkle with seasoning. Bring 2 edges of the foil up over the fish. Holding edges together, fold down toward fish, leaving space for air expansion. Fold up other sides of foil. Transfer packets to baking sheets.

Bake about 20 minutes or until fish is firm to the touch and flakes easily. To test for doneness, using potholders, remove 1 packet and open to check the fish. When opening the packet, be aware of escaping steam, which is very hot.

Per Serving: Calories: 158; % Calories from fat: 36; Fat (gm): 6.2; Saturated fat (gm): 0.9; Cholesterol (mg): 65.5; Sodium (mg): 60; Protein (gm): 22.8; Carbohydrate (gm): 1.8
Exchanges: Milk: 0.0; Vegetable: 0.0; Fruit: 0.0; Bread: 0.0; Meat: 3.0; Fat: 0.0

Today's catfish is farm-raised and has a mild, sweet flavor that kids and adults enjoy.

⚙ LOW CARB

SOUTHERN-STYLE CATFISH

MAKES 4 SERVINGS, 1 FILLET PER SERVING

- $1/4$ cup yellow cornmeal
- 3 tablespoons all-purpose flour
- $1/4$ teaspoon salt
- $1/8$ teaspoon black pepper
- 4 catfish fillets (4 ounces each), rinsed and patted dry
  Butter-flavored nonstick cooking spray

Combine cornmeal, flour, salt, and pepper on a sheet of waxed paper. Coat fillets in the cornmeal mixture.

Lightly coat a nonstick frying pan with cooking spray. Pan-fry the fish over medium heat until golden brown on each side, turning once with a spatula, about 3 minutes each side or until fish is opaque, firm to the touch, and flakes easily.

SERVING SUGGESTION: Garnish with lemon wedges.

Per Serving: Calories: 201; % Calories from fat: 41; Fat (gm): 8.9; Saturated fat (gm): 2; Cholesterol (mg): 52.9; Sodium (mg): 208; Protein (gm): 18.9; Carbohydrate (gm): 10.3
Exchanges: Milk: 0.0; Vegetable: 0.0; Fruit: 0.0; Bread: 1.0; Meat: 2.0; Fat: 0.5

Serve these crab cakes with lemon wedges and low-fat tartar sauce.

◔ LOW CARB
🐄 LOW FAT

CRAB CAKES

MAKES 8 SMALL CRAB CAKES, 1 PER APPETIZER SERVING

- 1/4 cup egg substitute
- 2 tablespoons fat-free mayonnaise
- 1 teaspoon dry mustard
- 2 cans (4 1/4 ounces each) crabmeat, or fresh crabmeat, about 1/2 pound
- 3/4 cup fresh whole-wheat bread crumbs
- Salt, to taste
- 1/8 teaspoon black pepper
- Butter-flavored nonstick cooking spray

Beat together egg substitute, mayonnaise, and mustard in a large bowl. Stir in crabmeat, crumbs, salt, and pepper.

Shape mixture into 8 small cakes. Place cakes on a plate and cover lightly with plastic wrap. Refrigerate at least 1 hour to firm up cakes.

Lightly coat a nonstick frying pan with cooking spray. Fry the cakes over medium heat, turning once, 3 to 4 minutes on each side.

TIP: For a main-dish serving, form 4 cakes instead of 8, remembering to double the nutrition information.

••

Per Serving: Calories: 69; % Calories from fat: 12; Fat (gm): 0.9; Saturated fat (gm): 0.2; Cholesterol (mg): 26.8; Sodium (mg): 344; Protein (gm): 6.5; Carbohydrate (gm): 8.1
Exchanges: Milk: 0.0; Vegetable: 0.0; Fruit: 0.0; Bread: 0.5; Meat: 1.0; Fat: 0.0

Serve these burgers on their own or with all of the trimmings: whole-wheat buns, lettuce, tomato, and pickle, as your eating plan allows.

○ LOW CARB

TERIYAKI SALMON BURGERS

MAKES 4 BURGERS, 1 BURGER PER SERVING

> 8 ounces skinless salmon fillet, cut into chunks
> 1/4 cup fresh bread crumbs
> 2 egg whites, slightly beaten
> 2 tablespoons reduced-sodium teriyaki sauce
> 2 tablespoons dried onion flakes
> 1/4 teaspoon black pepper
> Butter-flavored nonstick cooking spray

Grind the salmon to a coarse texture by pulsing briefly in a food processor or chop finely with a large, flat-bladed knife on a cutting board.

Combine ground salmon, bread crumbs, egg whites, teriyaki sauce, onion flakes, and black pepper in a bowl. Shape mixture into 4 burgers.

Lightly coat a nonstick frying pan with cooking spray. Cook the burgers over medium heat about 3 minutes on each side or until golden and cooked through.

Per Serving: Calories: 155; % Calories from fat: 37; Fat (gm): 6.3; Saturated fat (gm): 1.5; Cholesterol (mg): 37.4; Sodium (mg): 332; Protein (gm): 14.7; Carbohydrate (gm): 9
Exchanges: Milk: 0.0; Vegetable: 0.0; Fruit: 0.0; Bread: 0.5; Meat: 2.0; Fat: 0.0

⬧ **LOW CARB**

SIMPLE SALMON PIE

MAKES 6 SLICES, 1 SLICE PER SERVING

Nonstick cooking spray
1 can (16 ounces) salmon, drained
¼ cup water or low-sodium vegetable, or chicken, broth
2 egg whites, stiffly beaten
1 cup fresh whole-wheat bread crumbs
¼ cup chopped onion
1 tablespoon lemon juice
¼ teaspoon black pepper

Position rack in center of oven and preheat oven to 350 degrees F. Lightly coat a 9-inch pie plate with cooking spray.

Mash salmon in bowl, breaking up lumps. Add water. Gently stir in beaten egg whites, crumbs, onion, lemon juice, and black pepper.

Spoon mixture into prepared pan. Bake the salmon pie in center of the oven, 25 minutes or until lightly browned and cooked through. Can be served hot or cold.

Per Serving: Calories: 186; % Calories from fat: 26; Fat (gm): 5.1; Saturated fat (gm): 1.3; Cholesterol (mg): 29.5; Sodium (mg): 542; Protein (gm): 19.7; Carbohydrate (gm): 14
Exchanges: Milk: 0.0; Vegetable: 0.0; Fruit: 0.0; Bread: 1.0; Meat: 2.0; Fat: 0.0

When preparing couscous, follow package directions, omitting salt and fat, and use either water or reduced-sodium chicken broth. Whole-wheat couscous is available at natural foods stores.

🐮 LOW FAT
◇ LOW SODIUM

HALIBUT WITH COUSCOUS

MAKES 6 (1-CUP) SERVINGS

  1 cup flaked cooked halibut
  1 cup grated carrot
  2 cups cooked couscous
  2 cups prewashed baby spinach
  1/3 cup chopped chives
  1/4 cup balsamic vinegar
  1 tablespoon extra-virgin olive oil

Toss together the halibut, carrots, couscous, spinach, chives, vinegar, and oil.

Per Serving: Calories: 121; % Calories from fat: 22; Fat (gm): 3; Saturated fat (gm): 0.4; Cholesterol (mg): 7.7; Sodium (mg): 35; Protein (gm): 7.6; Carbohydrate (gm): 15.5
Exchanges: Milk: 0.0; Vegetable: 1.0; Fruit: 0.0; Bread: 0.5; Meat: 0.0; Fat: 1.0

CHAPTER NINE

Pizza, Pasta, and Sides

Try adding other toppings, such as artichokes or green peppers, to this simple pizza. Seasonings such as red pepper flakes, oregano, or fresh basil leaves add additional zip.

😋 LOW FAT

RUSTIC TOMATO AND CHEESE PIZZA

MAKES 8 SLICES, 1 SLICE PER SERVING

Olive oil-flavored nonstick cooking spray
1 can (10 ounces) refrigerated pizza crust dough
1 cup Rustic Tomato Sauce (recipe on Page 114)
$1/2$ cup (4 ounces) shredded, reduced-fat mozzarella cheese

Place an oven rack on the lowest shelf and preheat the oven to 425 degrees F. Lightly coat a 12-inch round nonstick pizza pan or a nonstick baking sheet with cooking spray. Press the dough onto the pizza pan or make a free-form shape on baking sheet. Spray the top of the dough after shaping.

Using the back of a spoon, spread the tomato sauce to within 1 inch of the rim of the dough. Sprinkle with cheese.

Bake the pizza on the lowest rack in the oven for 20 minutes or until crust is light golden brown and the topping is hot. Serve immediately.

TIP: As a time-saver, use a bottled or prepared refrigerated pizza sauce.

··

Per Serving: Calories: 119; % Calories from fat: 17; Fat (gm): 2.3; Saturated fat (gm): 0.8; Cholesterol (mg): 2.8; Sodium (mg): 243; Protein (gm): 5.3; Carbohydrate (gm): 19.8
Exchanges: Milk: 0.0; Vegetable: 1.0; Fruit: 0.0; Bread: 1.0; Meat: 0.0; Fat: 0.5

Calzone are simply mini pizzas that are folded in half.
Try different fillings, such as reduced-fat ricotta cheese
and spinach, anchovies, cooked mushrooms, or broccoli.

CALZONE

MAKES 6 CALZONE, 1 CALZONE PER SERVING

Olive oil-flavored cooking spray

1 can (10 ounces) refrigerated pizza crust dough or
homemade

3/4 cup Rustic Tomato Sauce (see Page 114) or bottled
reduced-sodium pizza sauce

1 cup fat-free ricotta cheese

2 ounces smoked sausage of pork and turkey

1 egg white, lightly beaten

Place oven rack on lowest shelf and preheat oven to 425 degrees F.
Lightly coat a baking sheet with cooking spray.

Roll out pizza dough on lightly floured board. Cut dough into 6
rounds. Lightly coat rounds with cooking spray. Using the back
of a spoon, spread tomato sauce over rounds to within 1/2 inch
of edge. Spread ricotta cheese on top. Arrange sausage on
rounds, covering only half of each.

Dampen edges with water and fold dough over to enclose filling.
Seal securely and press edges with tip of a fork. Using a spatula,
move each calzone to baking sheet. Brush with beaten egg white.

Bake for 20 minutes or until golden brown. Remove from oven
and serve immediately.

TIP: If using store-bought pizza sauce, look for brands with
reduced sodium.

Per Serving: Calories: 222; % Calories from fat: 30; Fat (gm): 7.5; Saturated fat (gm): 3.4;
Cholesterol (mg): 18.5; Sodium (mg): 423; Protein (gm): 11; Carbohydrate (gm): 27.6
Exchanges: Milk: 0.0; Vegetable: 2.0; Fruit: 0.0; Bread: 1.0; Meat: 1.0; Fat: 1.0

Focaccia, a traditional Italian flatbread, often has a dimpled surface made by repeatedly pressing a fingertip into the dough surface just before baking.

🐄 **LOW FAT**

FOCACCIA

MAKES 8 SQUARES, 1 SQUARE PER SERVING

> Olive oil-flavored nonstick cooking spray
> 1 can (10 ounces) pizza crust dough or homemade
> 3 cloves garlic, thinly sliced
> $\frac{1}{2}$ cup thinly sliced onion rings
> 2 tablespoons minced fresh rosemary
> $\frac{1}{8}$ teaspoon kosher salt (see note)

Place oven rack in center of oven and preheat oven to 500 degrees F. Lightly coat an 8-inch square baking pan with cooking spray.

Stretch and shape the dough to fit the pan. Lightly coat the dough with cooking spray. Sprinkle the dough with garlic. Arrange onion over top of dough. Sprinkle with rosemary and salt. Lightly spray top again. Dimple the surface with fingertip if desired.

Bake for 5 to 8 minutes or until lightly golden. Cut into 8 squares and serve warm or at room temperature.

NOTE: Kosher salt is an additive-free, coarse-grained salt that adds texture and flavor to focaccia. Large-grained sea salt can also be used. Many cooks prefer kosher and sea salt to regular salt for its flavor and texture. It can be omitted for those on a salt-restricted diet.

Per Serving: Calories: 96; % Calories from fat: 12; Fat (gm): 1.3; Saturated fat (gm): 0.3; Cholesterol (mg): 0; Sodium (mg): 232; Protein (gm): 3.2; Carbohydrate (gm): 17.8
Exchanges: Milk: 0.0; Vegetable: 0.0; Fruit: 0.0; Bread: 1.0; Meat: 0.0; Fat: 0.0

This unusual pizza is a family after-school favorite. Matzo is large unleavened bread that is like a big cracker. It is available in the kosher food aisle of most supermarkets.

🐮 LOW FAT

ETHAN'S MATZO PIZZA

MAKES 2 SERVINGS

1 sheet matzo, broken in half
$1/3$ cup jarred pasta sauce
$1/2$ cup nonfat mozzarella cheese

Preheat the oven to 425 degrees F. or use the microwave on HIGH. Using the back of a spoon, spread the pizza sauce over the matzo. Sprinkle with the cheese.

Place the matzo on a nonstick baking sheet and bake in the center of the oven for 5 minutes or until the cheese melts. If using a microwave, cook on HIGH for 1 minute or until the cheese melts.

Per Serving: Calories: 114; % Calories from fat: 10; Fat (gm): 1.3; Saturated fat (gm): 0.2; Cholesterol (mg): 0; Sodium (mg): 324; Protein (gm): 9; Carbohydrate (gm): 15.7
Exchanges: Milk: 0.0; Vegetable: 0.0; Fruit: 0.0; Bread: 1.0; Meat: 0.0; Fat: 0.5

This whimsical pizza is fun to make and eat. Use extra dough scraps to make scarves and hats for the snowman. You can prepare the crust ahead of time: cover and freeze.

SNOWMAN PIZZAS

MAKES 6 SERVINGS, 1 SNOWMAN PER SERVING

- 1 can (10 ounces) pizza crust dough or homemade
- 1 tablespoon cornmeal for baking sheets
- 1 1/2 cups part-skim ricotta cheese
- 1/4 chopped tomatoes or reconstituted dried tomatoes, chopped
- 1/4 cup marinated artichoke hearts, drained and separated
- 1 cup thinly sliced green pepper

Roll out the dough on lightly floured cutting board. Cut into 6 3-inch circles and 6 5-inch circles. Press smaller and larger circles together to make 6 snowman shapes, wetting the adjoining edges so they stick together. Make scarves and hats from the scraps.

Sprinkle nonstick baking sheets with cornmeal. Lift snowmen with a spatula and set on baking pans.

Position oven shelf in lowest position and preheat the oven to 425 degrees F. Pierce each snowman in several places with the tines of a fork. Let rise 10 minutes. Bake for about 15 minutes or until firm to the touch. Cool.

Spread the cheese over pizzas. Use tomatoes for eyes, mouths, and buttons. Use the artichoke hearts and pepper slices for hats and scarves.

Bake pizzas again for about 5 minutes or until the toppings are hot.

Per Serving: Calories: 226; % Calories from fat: 31; Fat (gm): 7.7; Saturated fat (gm): 3.6; Cholesterol (mg): 19.1; Sodium (mg): 364; Protein (gm): 11.3; Carbohydrate (gm): 28.1
Exchanges: Milk: 0.0; Vegetable: 0.0; Fruit: 0.0; Bread: 2.0; Meat: 1.0; Fat: 1.0

When shopping for pasta sauce, always read the ingredients and nutrition labels and look for those lowest in fat, sugar, and sodium.

🐮 LOW FAT

LASAGNA ROLLUPS

MAKES 6 SERVINGS, 1 ROLLUP PER SERVING

Olive oil-flavored nonstick cooking spray

1 container (15 ounces) reduced-fat ricotta cheese

1 package (10 ounces) frozen chopped spinach, defrosted and squeezed dry

1/4 cup egg substitute or 2 eggs

6 spinach or plain lasagna noodles, cooked and drained

1 cup spaghetti sauce, bottled or homemade (recipe on page 110)

Position oven rack in center of oven and preheat oven to 350 degrees F. Lightly coat an ovenproof dish or casserole with cooking spray.

Combine the ricotta, spinach, and egg substitute in a mixing bowl.

Spread about 1/2 cup of the ricotta mixture down the length of each noodle. Roll up each noodle jelly-roll style. Set rolls, edge side up, in baking dish. Drizzle the spaghetti sauce over the rolls.

Bake for 30 minutes.

SERVING SUGGESTION: Offer shredded Parmesan cheese at the table.

Per Serving: Calories: 161; % Calories from fat: 14; Fat (gm): 2.6; Saturated fat (gm): 1.4; Cholesterol (mg): 12.4; Sodium (mg): 286; Protein (gm): 15.5; Carbohydrate (gm): 20
Exchanges: Milk: 0.0; Vegetable: 1.0; Fruit: 0.0; Bread: 1.0; Meat: 1.5; Fat: 0.0

This is a simple dish to make for kids. Let them make the face with the vegetables. As a shortcut, use canned, drained carrots and green beans.

🐮 LOW FAT

MACARONI FACE

MAKES 8 (½-CUP) SERVINGS

12 ounces uncooked whole-wheat macaroni
⅓ cup fat-free French salad dressing
½ cup sliced cooked carrots
½ cup cooked green beans

Cook macaroni according to the package directions, omitting salt. Drain.

Toss together macaroni and dressing in mixing bowl. Divide macaroni among 8 individual serving bowls or plates.

Make a face with the macaroni, using carrot rounds for eyes, ears, and a nose and green beans for a mouth and hair.

Per Serving: Calories: 160; % Calories from fat: 3; Fat (gm): 0.6; Saturated fat (gm): 0.1; Cholesterol (mg): 0; Sodium (mg): 204; Protein (gm): 6.4; Carbohydrate (gm): 34.5
Exchanges: Milk: 0.0; Vegetable: 0.0; Fruit: 0.0; Bread: 2.5; Meat: 0.0; Fat: 0.0

Pan frying this pasta dish adds a delicious crispness to the crust.

PAN-FRIED CHEESE RAVIOLI

MAKES 8 (½-CUP) SERVINGS

2 packages (9 ounces each) refrigerated low-fat
cheese ravioli

Butter-flavored nonstick cooking spray

Cook ravioli according to package directions, omitting salt. Drain.

Place ravioli in a single layer on paper towels.

Lightly coat a nonstick frying pan with cooking spray. Cook ravioli until golden on each side, turning once, about 2 minutes per side.

SERVING SUGGESTION: Serve with Barbecue Sauce (recipe on Page 111). If using store-bought sauce, read ingredient and nutrition labels and look for those lowest in fat, sugar, and sodium.

Per Serving: Calories: 174; % Calories from fat: 19; Fat (gm): 3.6; Saturated fat (gm): 1.4; Cholesterol (mg): 43.5; Sodium (mg): 246; Protein (gm): 9.4; Carbohydrate (gm): 25.4
Exchanges: Milk: 0.0; Vegetable: 0.0; Fruit: 0.0; Bread: 2.0; Meat: 1.0; Fat: 0.5

Brown rice is a good nutritional choice because it is rich in magnesium, phosphorus, and selenium and has vitamin B-6, dietary fiber, thiamin, and niacin. Brown rice takes longer to cook than white rice, but instant brown rice takes only 10 minutes.

🐮 LOW FAT

FRIED BROWN RICE

MAKES 8 (1-CUP) SERVINGS

Canola oil-flavored nonstick cooking spray
1/2 cup chopped onion
1/2 cup grated carrot
3 cups cooked brown rice
2 cups fresh bean sprouts, rinsed and drained
1 package (10 ounces) frozen green peas, thawed
3 tablespoons soy sauce

Lightly coat a nonstick frying pan or wok with cooking spray.

Cook the onions over medium heat, stirring constantly, for about 5 minutes or until tender. Lightly spray the pan again. Add the rice, carrots, bean sprouts, green peas, and soy sauce. Cook, stirring constantly, for about 2 minutes or until hot.

SERVING SUGGESTION: For a hearty main dish, add 1 lightly beaten egg and/or 1 cup diced tofu when cooking the rice and vegetable mixture.

Per Serving: Calories: 127; % Calories from fat: 6; Fat (gm): 0.8; Saturated fat (gm): 0.2; Cholesterol (mg): 0; Sodium (mg): 425; Protein (gm): 5; Carbohydrate (gm): 25.5
Exchanges: Milk: 0.0; Vegetable: 0.0; Fruit: 0.0; Bread: 2.0; Meat: 0.0; Fat: 0.0

Barley is a hardy grain that has been used since Stone Age times in foods ranging from cereals and breads to beer. It is a nice change of pace from rice.

🐄 LOW FAT
◇ LOW SODIUM

BARLEY AND VEGETABLES

MAKES 8 (¾-CUP) SERVINGS

Butter-flavored nonstick cooking spray

1 package (1 pound) frozen Italian-blend vegetables

1 cup water

1 ½ cups uncooked quick-cooking barley

2 teaspoons Cajun seasoning mix

Lightly coat a large nonstick frying pan with cooking spray. Cook the vegetables over medium heat, stirring often, for about 5 minutes or until the vegetables are tender.

Stir in water, barley, and seasonings. Bring mixture to a boil over high heat. Reduce heat to medium-low. Cover and simmer for 10 minutes or until barley is tender.

Per Serving: Calories: 142; % Calories from fat: 5; Fat (gm): 0.8; Saturated fat (gm): 0.2; Cholesterol (mg): 0; Sodium (mg): 24; Protein (gm): 5; Carbohydrate (gm): 28.7
Exchanges: Milk: 0.0; Vegetable: 0.0; Fruit: 0.0; Bread: 2.0; Meat: 0.0; Fat: 0.0

CHAPTER TEN

Sauces

For a thicker sauce, remove $^1/_2$ cup of the sauce and mix it with $1^1/_2$ teaspoons cornstarch. Return the mixture to the pan and continue cooking, stirring often, until the sauce thickens slightly. If you want a richer sauce, substitute 1 cup of fat-free half-and-half for 1 cup of the water. The sauce is even better the next day.

⚬ **LOW CARB**
⚬ **LOW FAT**
◇ **LOW SODIUM**

CHOCOLATE SAUCE

MAKES 1½ CUPS SAUCE, OR 12 SERVINGS OF 2 TABLESPOONS

- $^1/_2$ cup cocoa powder
- $1^1/_2$ cups water
- $^1/_3$ cup sugar
- $1^1/_2$ teaspoons vanilla

Whisk the cocoa with $^3/_4$ cup of the cold water in a saucepan over medium heat. Add the remaining $^3/_4$ cup of water and the sugar. Bring the mixture to a boil. Reduce the heat to a simmer. Cook for 3 minutes stirring often.

Remove sauce from heat and cool. Stir in the vanilla.

Spoon the sauce into a container and refrigerate covered until ready to serve. Stir before serving.

Per Serving: Calories: 30; % Calories from fat: 11; Fat (gm): 0.5; Saturated fat (gm): 0.3; Cholesterol (mg): 0; Sodium (mg): 1; Protein (gm): 0.7; Carbohydrate (gm): 7.4
Exchanges: Milk: 0.0; Vegetable: 0.0; Fruit: 0.0; Bread: 0.5; Meat: 0.0; Fat: 0.0

Salsa is one on those recipes that you can customize for your family's flavor preferences. The following recipe can be doubled. For spicier salsa, add seeded, minced jalapeño or other chile to taste.

🔥 **LOW CARB**
🐄 **LOW FAT**
◇ **LOW SODIUM**

CHUNKY SALSA

MAKES ABOUT 1¾ CUPS, OR 4 SERVINGS

- 1 cup chopped fresh tomatoes
- ³/₄ cup chopped onions
- ¹/₂ cup chopped fresh cilantro
- 2 tablespoons lime juice

In a bowl, combine tomato, onion, cilantro, and lime juice. Cover and refrigerate until serving time.

Per Serving: Calories: 23; % Calories from fat: 7; Fat (gm): 0.2; Saturated fat (gm): 0; Cholesterol (mg): 0; Sodium (mg): 5; Protein (gm): 0.8; Carbohydrate (gm): 5.4
Exchanges: Milk: 0.0; Vegetable: 1.0; Fruit: 0.0; Bread: 0.0; Meat: 0.0; Fat: 0.0

Cooking tomatoes releases an important nutrient called lycopene, which is thought to have significant heart-protective health benefits. Keep cooked tomato sauce on hand in the refrigerator or freezer to use on pasta and in casseroles, as a dipper with cut-up vegetables, and as a pizza topper or bread spread.

◌ **LOW CARB**
🐾 **LOW FAT**
◇ **LOW SODIUM**

10-MINUTE SPAGHETTI SAUCE

MAKES 8 (1-CUP) SERVINGS

Olive oil-flavored nonstick cooking spray

1 cup chopped onions

1 cup chopped zucchini

1 cup grated carrots

1 can (28 ounces) reduced-sodium crushed tomatoes, including juice

2 cans (8 ounces each) reduced-sodium tomato sauce

1 tablespoon Italian seasoning

Lightly coat a nonstick saucepan with cooking spray. Heat over medium heat. Add onions, zucchini, and carrots and cook, partially covered and stirring occasionally, for 5 minutes or until tender.

Stir in tomatoes with juice, tomato sauce, and seasoning. Bring sauce to a boil. Reduce heat to brisk simmer and cook, uncovered, for 5 minutes.

....

Per Serving: Calories: 51; % Calories from fat: 5; Fat (gm): 0.3; Saturated fat (gm): 0; Cholesterol (mg): 0; Sodium (mg): 43; Protein (gm): 2.3; Carbohydrate (gm): 9.7
Exchanges: Milk: 0.0; Vegetable: 2.0; Fruit: 0.0; Bread: 0.0; Meat: 0.0; Fat: 0.0

Traditional barbecue sauce is high in carbohydrates and sodium, making it unsuitable for most eating plans. Our version lightens up considerably, thanks to spoonable brown sugar substitute. If your supermarket does not carry brown sugar substitute, use a spoonable granulated sugar substitute or sugar-free maple-flavored syrup. If using syrup, cook the sauce a little longer to desired thickness.

◔ **LOW CARB**
🐄 **LOW FAT**
◇ **LOW SODIUM**

BARBECUE SAUCE

MAKES 8 SERVINGS, 2 TABLESPOONS PER SERVING

Butter-flavored nonstick cooking spray
$1/2$ cup chopped onion
$1/2$ cup chopped, seeded green bell pepper
$1/2$ cup water
$1/3$ cup ketchup
1 teaspoon barbecue spice mix
$2\,1/2$ tablespoons red wine vinegar
2 teaspoons Worcestershire sauce
3 tablespoons spoonable brown sugar substitute

Lightly coat a saucepan with cooking spray. Cook onions and green pepper over medium heat, stirring occasionally, for 5 minutes or until tender.

Stir in water, ketchup, spice mix, vinegar, Worcestershire sauce, and sugar substitute. Simmer for 5 minutes.

Spoon sauce into covered container and store in refrigerator. Stir before serving.

Per Serving: Calories: 20; % Calories from fat: 3; Fat (gm): 0.1; Saturated fat (gm): 0; Cholesterol (mg): 0; Sodium (mg): 126; Protein (gm): 0.4; Carbohydrate (gm): 5
Exchanges: Milk: 0.0; Vegetable: 0.0; Fruit: 0.0; Bread: 0.0; Meat: 0.0; Fat: 0.0

This is an excellent all-purpose sauce to have on hand. It is especially good on fish such as salmon and can also be used as a bread spread or dip.

⏱ **LOW CARB**
🐄 **LOW FAT**

YOGURT DILL SAUCE

MAKES 8 SERVINGS, 3 TABLESPOONS PER SERVING

   1 cup nonfat plain yogurt
   $1/2$ cup fat-free mayonnaise
   1 teaspoon minced garlic
   2 teaspoons dill seeds or 2 tablespoons minced fresh dill

Mix together the yogurt, mayonnaise, garlic, and dill in a small bowl.

Cover and store in the refrigerator. Stir before serving.

Per Serving: Calories: 29; % Calories from fat: 4; Fat (gm): 0.1; Saturated fat (gm): 0; Cholesterol (mg): 0.6; Sodium (mg): 144; Protein (gm): 1.9; Carbohydrate (gm): 4.8
Exchanges: Milk: 0.0; Vegetable: 0.0; Fruit: 0.0; Bread: 0.5; Meat: 0.0; Fat: 0.0

This sauce is perfect for both pasta and pizza. It can be stored in a covered container in the refrigerator up to one week or can be frozen for up to three weeks.

⚬ LOW CARB
♨ LOW FAT
◇ LOW SODIUM

MARINARA SAUCE

MAKES 4 (½-CUP) SERVINGS

Olive oil-flavored nonstick cooking spray
½ cup chopped onion
½ teaspoon minced garlic or garlic powder
1 can (14½ ounces) reduced-sodium Italian-style crushed tomatoes, with liquid
1 can (6 ounces) reduced-sodium tomato paste
1 tablespoon Italian seasoning

Lightly coat a large nonstick saucepan with cooking spray. Cook onions and garlic over medium heat 4 to 5 minutes, stirring occasionally and spraying once, until onions are soft.

Stir in tomatoes with liquid, tomato paste, and seasonings. Simmer 5 minutes or until sauce thicken slightly, stirring occasionally.

Serve immediately or pour cooled sauce into a covered container and store in the refrigerator.

Per Serving: Calories: 65; % Calories from fat: 4; Fat (gm): 0.3; Saturated fat (gm): 0; Cholesterol (mg): 0; Sodium (mg): 64; Protein (gm): 2.7; Carbohydrate (gm): 13.5
Exchanges: Milk: 0.0; Vegetable: 3.0; Fruit: 0.0; Bread: 0.0; Meat: 0.0; Fat: 0.0

This is another sauce that does double duty as a pasta or pizza topper. Try it over steamed vegetables for a change of pace.

⚬ **LOW CARB**

🐮 **LOW FAT**

◇ **LOW SODIUM**

RUSTIC TOMATO SAUCE

MAKES ABOUT 14 (¼-CUP) SERVINGS

Olive oil-flavored nonstick cooking spray

¼ cup water

4 cloves garlic, minced

1¼ cups chopped onions

1 can (28 ounces) reduced-sodium plum tomatoes, including juice

1 can (6 ounces) reduced-sodium tomato paste

2 teaspoons ground oregano

Lightly coat a large nonstick saucepan with cooking spray and warm the pan over medium heat. Add water, garlic, onions, and tomatoes. Cook for 2 minutes. Stir in tomato paste and oregano.

Bring the sauce to a boil. Reduce the heat to medium-low and simmer uncovered for 25 minutes, stirring occasionally. Sauce will thicken as it cooks. Remove sauce from heat. Use immediately or cool and refrigerate.

TIP: For a chunkier sauce, add ½ cup diced celery.

Per Serving: Calories: 28; % Calories from fat: 5; Fat (gm): 0.2; Saturated fat (gm): 0; Cholesterol (mg): 0; Sodium (mg): 17; Protein (gm): 1.2; Carbohydrate (gm): 6.5
Exchanges: Milk: 0.0; Vegetable: 1.0; Fruit: 0.0; Bread: 0.0; Meat: 0.0; Fat: 0.0

This sauce is traditionally made with coconut milk, which is high in fat. We've reduced the fat by using evaporated skim milk and reduced-fat peanut butter. The sauce can also be used as a dipper for vegetables and as a topper for rice dishes. Spice it up if you wish with a dash of cayenne pepper or hot sauce.

🍎 **LOW CARB**
🐾 **LOW FAT**
◇ **LOW SODIUM**

THAI PEANUT SAUCE

MAKES 8 SERVINGS, 2 TABLESPOONS PER SERVING

$1/2$ cup evaporated skim milk (not condensed)
$1/4$ cup reduced-fat peanut butter
$1/4$ cup chopped onion
1 teaspoon lemon juice
1 teaspoon chopped gingerroot or powdered ginger

Whisk together milk, peanut butter, onion, lemon juice, and ginger in saucepan. Simmer the mixture a few minutes until smooth and heated through.

Serve hot or pour into a container and refrigerate covered until ready to serve.

SERVING SUGGESTION: Dress up the sauce for company with a garnish of chopped peanuts and cilantro leaves.

Per Serving: Calories: 62; % Calories from fat: 42; Fat (gm): 3; Saturated fat (gm): 0.6; Cholesterol (mg): 0.6; Sodium (mg): 81; Protein (gm): 3.3; Carbohydrate (gm): 6.1
Exchanges: Milk: 0.0; Vegetable: 0.0; Fruit: 0.0; Bread: 0.5; Meat: 0.0; Fat: 0.5

CHAPTER ELEVEN

Baked Goods

For extra flavor and crunch, top the bread sticks with sesame seeds or poppy seeds or a mixture of both.

🐮 LOW FAT

BREAD STICKS

MAKES 16 STICKS, OR 8 SERVINGS OF 2 STICKS

　　Nonstick cooking spray
1　can (10 ounces) pizza crust dough or homemade
$1/4$　cup grated Parmesan cheese
1　tablespoon dried rosemary

Preheat oven to 400 degrees F. Lightly coat a baking sheet with nonstick cooking spray.

Cut dough into 16 equal pieces using a sharp knife. Roll each piece into sticks the thickness and length of a pencil. Place the dough sticks on the baking sheet, straightening as necessary.

Lightly coat the dough with cooking spray. Combine the cheese and rosemary in a small bowl. Sprinkle the dough sticks with the mixture.

Bake for 15 to 20 minutes until golden brown. Cooled bread sticks can be wrapped for storage in the freezer or in a cool, dry place.

SERVING SUGGESTION: For a sweet topping, omit the Parmesan cheese and rosemary. Bake the bread sticks as directed. When the bread sticks come out of the oven, sprinkle with a mixture of 1 tablespoon cinnamon and 2 to 3 packets sugar substitute of your choice.

....

Per Serving: Calories: 103; % Calories from fat: 18; Fat (gm): 2.1; Saturated fat (gm): 0.8; Cholesterol (mg): 2; Sodium (mg): 241; Protein (gm): 4.1; Carbohydrate (gm): 16.9
Exchanges: Milk: 0.0; Vegetable: 0.0; Fruit: 0.0; Bread: 1.0; Meat: 0.0; Fat: 0.5

To make cornbread instead of muffins, pour the batter into a lightly sprayed baking pan or iron skillet and bake at 400 degrees F. for about 20 minutes.

☙ LOW FAT

BUTTERMILK CORN MUFFINS

MAKES 12 MUFFINS, 1 MUFFIN PER SERVING

Butter-flavored nonstick cooking spray

1 1/4 cups all-purpose flour

2 teaspoons baking powder

3 tablespoons sugar

3 tablespoons reduced-fat margarine, melted

1 cup yellow cornmeal

1 1/4 cups low-fat buttermilk

1/2 cup egg substitute or 2 eggs

Position rack in center of the oven and preheat oven to 400 degrees F. Lightly coat a muffin pan with cooking spray.

Combine flour, baking powder, and sugar in large mixing bowl. Stir in margarine and cornmeal. Stir in buttermilk and egg substitute. Stir only until just mixed, taking care not to overmix.

Pour the batter into muffin pan. Bake for about 20 minutes or until golden, and toothpick or cake tester inserted in center of muffin comes out clean and dry.

Cool the muffins on wire rack for 5 minutes before turning muffins out of pan.

TIP: For extra flavor and texture, add 1 cup fresh, frozen, or canned, drained corn kernels to the batter.

Per Serving: Calories: 124; % Calories from fat: 15; Fat (gm): 2.1; Saturated fat (gm): 0.4; Cholesterol (mg): 1; Sodium (mg): 165; Protein (gm): 4; Carbohydrate (gm): 22.4
Exchanges: Milk: 0.0; Vegetable: 0.0; Fruit: 0.0; Bread: 1.5; Meat: 0.0; Fat: 0.5

It is easy and fun to make your own pretzels, and children love to help twist the dough. Delicious alone, you can also serve them with mustard, low-fat plain yogurt, or nonfat ranch-style dressing.

♨ **LOW CARB**
◈ **LOW SODIUM**

PRETZELS

MAKES 24 PRETZELS, OR 12 SERVINGS OF 2 PRETZELS

   1 $1/3$ cups sifted all-purpose flour
   2 tablespoons sugar
   $1/2$ cup margarine, chilled
   $1/4$ cup egg substitute
   1 egg white, lightly beaten
   $1/2$ cup toasted sesame seeds

Combine flour and sugar in a large mixing bowl. Cut in margarine with a pastry blender, electric mixer, or fingertips. Stir in egg substitute and blend well. Form dough into a ball. Flatten dough slightly on a lightly floured surface. Cover in plastic wrap and chill for 2 hours.

Pull off pieces of dough about a tablespoon in size. Roll out each piece on a lightly floured surface to form 10-inch ropes. Form rope rings, then cross ends and twist to make pretzel shapes. Place on nonstick baking sheets. Chill for 20 minutes.

Preheat oven to 375 degrees F. Brush tops of pretzels with egg white. Sprinkle with sesame seeds.

Bake for 10 to 12 minutes or until golden. Remove from baking sheet and cool on a wire rack.

TIP: Substitute an equal amount of chopped almonds, a sprinkling of kosher salt, or cinnamon-sugar for the sesame seeds.

....

Per Serving: Calories: 168; % Calories from fat: 59; Fat (gm): 11.1; Saturated fat (gm): 2.1; Cholesterol (mg): 17.7; Sodium (mg): 99; Protein (gm): 3.4; Carbohydrate (gm): 14.2
Exchanges: Milk: 0.0; Vegetable: 0.0; Fruit: 0.0; Bread: 1.0; Meat: 0.0; Fat: 2.0

Lighter-than-air biscuits require a light touch when it comes to mixing. If using your fingertips to cut the margarine into the flour, work quickly and lightly. A light touch also helps when stirring the yogurt and cheese into the flour mixture.

⏱ **LOW CARB**

CHEDDAR BISCUITS

MAKES 18 BISCUITS, 1 BISCUIT PER SERVING

Butter-flavored nonstick cooking spray

1/2 cup margarine

2 cups self-rising flour (see note)

1 1/4 cups nonfat plain yogurt

1 cup (4 ounces) shredded reduced-fat mild Cheddar cheese

Preheat oven to 450 degrees F. Lightly coat a nonstick baking sheet with cooking spray.

Cut margarine into flour using pastry blender, 2 knives, or fingertips until mixture is crumbly. Stir in yogurt and cheese, mixing lightly just until ingredients are combined.

Drop batter by the tablespoonful onto baking sheet. Bake 10 to 12 minutes or until biscuits are golden.

NOTE: If self-rising flour is not available where you shop, make your own by adding 1 tablespoon of salt and 5 tablespoons of baking powder to every 8 cups of all-purpose flour.

Per Serving: Calories: 128; % Calories from fat: 50; Fat (gm): 6.8; Saturated fat (gm): 2.3; Cholesterol (mg): 4.8; Sodium (mg): 243; Protein (gm): 3.9; Carbohydrate (gm): 11.7
Exchanges: Milk: 0.0; Vegetable: 0.0; Fruit: 0.0; Bread: 1.0; Meat: 0.0; Fat: 1.0

Fresh, canned, or frozen blueberries work well in this recipe. If using frozen berries, defrost before using.

BLUEBERRY MUFFINS

MAKES 12 MUFFINS OR 24 MINI-MUFFINS, 1 MUFFIN OR
2 MINI-MUFFINS PER SERVING

Butter-flavored nonstick cooking spray
$1/4$ cup margarine, at room temperature
$1/3$ cup sugar
2 eggs
2 cups sifted all-purpose flour
4 teaspoons baking powder
$2/3$ cup skim milk
$3/4$ cup fresh blueberries

Preheat oven to 400 degrees F. Lightly coat a nonstick muffin pan with cooking spray.

Cream the margarine and sugar together in a bowl with an electric mixer. Mix in the eggs.

Mix together the flour and baking powder in a separate bowl. Add the flour mixture alternately with milk to the margarine mixture. Gently stir in berries.

Spoon the batter into the muffin pan, filling cups $2/3$ full. Bake for 20 minutes or until cake tester or wooden pick inserted into center of a muffin comes out clean and dry.

Per Serving: Calories: 153; % Calories from fat: 29; Fat (gm): 4.9; Saturated fat (gm): 1.1; Cholesterol (mg): 35.7; Sodium (mg): 225; Protein (gm): 3.8; Carbohydrate (gm): 23.7
Exchanges: Milk: 0.0; Vegetable: 0.0; Fruit: 0.0; Bread: 1.5; Meat: 0.0; Fat: 1.0

CHAPTER TWELVE

Desserts

It's possible to still enjoy rich, chewy brownies as long as you keep the serving size reasonable.

🐮 **LOW FAT**
◇ **LOW SODIUM**

JENNY'S BROWNIES

MAKES 16 BROWNIES, 1 BROWNIE PER SERVING

Butter-flavored nonstick cooking spray
$1/3$ cup reduced-fat margarine, melted and slightly cooled
$1/3$ cup cocoa powder
$1/2$ cup egg substitute
$3/4$ cup cake flour
$1/2$ cup sugar
$1/2$ teaspoon baking powder
$1 1/2$ teaspoons vanilla

Position oven rack in center and preheat oven to 350 degrees F. Lightly coat an 8-inch square nonstick baking pan with cooking spray.

Whisk together margarine and cocoa in bowl. Blend in egg substitute.

Sift together flour, sugar, and baking powder in large bowl. Stir margarine mixture into flour mixture. Add vanilla.

Pour batter into pan. Bake for 25 minutes or until cake tester or toothpick inserted in center comes out dry and clean.

Cool brownies in pan. Cut into squares in pan.

....

Per Serving: Calories: 67; % Calories from fat: 27; Fat (gm): 2.1; Saturated fat (gm): 0.4; Cholesterol (mg): 0; Sodium (mg): 75; Protein (gm): 1.5; Carbohydrate (gm): 11.2
Exchanges: Milk: 0.0; Vegetable: 0.0; Fruit: 0.0; Bread: 1.0; Meat: 0.0; Fat: 0.0

If you don't have time to make a crust from scratch, purchase one from the supermarket. Read the ingredient and nutritional labels to find one with the lowest and least amount of hydrogenated fat.

BAKED ALASKA PIE

MAKES 8 SLICES, 1 SLICE PER SERVING

1 9-inch graham cracker crust (recipe on Page 126)
5 cups no-sugar-added ice cream
4 egg whites
$1/2$ teaspoon cream of tartar
$1/3$ cup sugar

Refrigerate the crust for at least 20 minutes.

Remove the ice cream from the freezer and allow it to stand and soften a few minutes. Stir ice cream as it softens. Spread ice cream in the crust. Cover the filled crust with aluminum foil and freeze until solid.

When ready to serve, preheat oven to 500 degrees F. Beat egg whites with cream of tartar until soft peaks form. Sprinkle sugar over egg whites. Continue beating until stiff. Mound meringue over ice cream. Spread the meringue to the edges of the crust, making sure the meringue touches the crust to seal the edges.

Set the pie on a baking sheet. Bake for 2 to 3 minutes or just until the tips of meringue are golden brown. Cut into 8 slices and serve immediately.

Per Serving: Calories: 251; % Calories from fat: 32; Fat (gm): 8.9; Saturated fat (gm): 2.9; Cholesterol (mg): 12.5; Sodium (mg): 299; Protein (gm): 7.2; Carbohydrate (gm): 35.5
Exchanges: Milk: 0.0; Vegetable: 0.0; Fruit: 0.0; Bread: 2.5; Meat: 0.0; Fat: 1.5

For a change of pace, make the crust with gingersnaps instead of graham crackers. The easiest way to make graham cracker or gingersnap crumbs is in the food processor or blender.

GRAHAM CRACKER CRUST

MAKES 1 (9-INCH) PIE CRUST TO SERVE 8

    5 tablespoons reduced-calorie margarine

1 $1/4$ cups graham cracker crumbs

    $1/2$ teaspoon ground cinnamon

Preheat oven to 350 degrees F. Stir the margarine, crumbs, and cinnamon together in a bowl. Press the mixture firmly into the bottom and up the sides of a 9-inch pie pan.

Bake 10 minutes. Cool on wire rack. Cut into 8 slices.

Per Serving: Calories: 98; % Calories from fat: 48; Fat (gm): 5.2; Saturated fat (gm): 1; Cholesterol (mg): 0; Sodium (mg): 209; Protein (gm): 1.7; Carbohydrate (gm): 11
Exchanges: Milk: 0.0; Vegetable: 0.0; Fruit: 0.0; Bread: 1.0; Meat: 0.0; Fat: 1.0

To peel peaches, drop in boiling water for about 30 seconds. Remove with a slotted spoon. When cool enough to handle, slip off the skins. For extra flavor in the pie, add 1/4 teaspoon ground nutmeg and/or 1/2 teaspoon ground cinnamon.

PEACH YOGURT PIE

MAKES 8 SERVINGS, 1 SLICE PER SERVING

1 (9-inch) Graham Cracker Crust (recipe on Page 126) or gingersnap crust

2 cups peeled, pitted, chopped fresh peaches

2 tablespoons no–sugar-added orange juice

2 tablespoons light brown sugar

4 cups plain low-fat yogurt

1 1/2 cups sugar-free, nondairy whipped topping

Refrigerate the crust for at least 20 minutes.

Gently toss together the peaches, orange juice, and sugar. Stir in the yogurt, then the whipped topping.

Mound the filling into the crust. Cover lightly with aluminum foil. Freeze the pie for 2 hours or until firm.

Just before serving, set the pie out at room temperature to soften slightly. Cut into 8 slices.

Per Serving: Calories: 257; % Calories from fat: 30; Fat (gm): 8.7; Saturated fat (gm): 3; Cholesterol (mg): 7.3; Sodium (mg): 304; Protein (gm): 8.7; Carbohydrate (gm): 35.9
Exchanges: Milk: 1.0; Vegetable: 0.0; Fruit: 0.0; Bread: 1.5; Meat: 0.0; Fat: 1.5

This recipe calls for thickened yogurt, which is sometimes called yogurt cheese. It resembles softened cream cheese or sour cream. Unflavored thickened yogurt is delicious with bread, fruit slices, or crackers. Add savory herbs and seasonings to plain thickened yogurt for extra flavor.

KEY LIME CHIFFON PIE

MAKES 8 SERVINGS, 1 SLICE PER SERVING

1 (9-inch) Graham Cracker Crust (recipe on Page 126)

4 cups no-sugar-added, low-fat thickened yogurt, drained (see note)

2 tablespoons grated lime peel

1 ½ cups sugar-free, nonfat whipped topping

Refrigerate the crust for at least 20 minutes.

In a deep bowl, mix together yogurt, lime peel, and whipped topping. Mound the filling into the crust. Cover the pie lightly with aluminum foil. Freeze for 2 hours or until firm.

Set pie on counter at room temperature until it softens slightly but does not defrost. Cut into 8 slices.

NOTE: To drain yogurt, line a strainer with a double layer of cheesecloth, or fit the strainer with a paper coffee filter. Place the strainer in a bowl with enough room underneath for drainage. Put the yogurt in the strainer and cover the strainer with a plate or plastic wrap. (Do not use custard-style or whipped yogurt.) Refrigerate for one day while it drains. Discard the liquid in the bowl and scrape the thickened yogurt off the cheesecloth.

Per Serving: Calories: 246; % Calories from fat: 24; Fat (gm): 6.5; Saturated fat (gm): 1.8; Cholesterol (mg): 4.9; Sodium (mg): 288; Protein (gm): 7; Carbohydrate (gm): 39.1
Exchanges: Milk: 0.0; Vegetable: 0.0; Fruit: 0.0; Bread: 2.5; Meat: 0.0; Fat: 1.0

BLUEBERRY MOUSSE PIE

- 1 (9-inch) Graham Cracker Crust (recipe on Page 126)
- 2 packages (3 ounces each) sugar-free, low-calorie raspberry gelatin
- 2 cups boiling water
- 1/2 cup cold water
- 2 cups no-sugar-added, low-fat blueberry yogurt
- 1 cup fresh blueberries

Refrigerate the crust for at least 20 minutes.

Sprinkle the gelatin into a mixing bowl. Stir in boiling water and mix until gelatin dissolves completely. Stir in cold water and set gelatin aside at room temperature until it begins to thicken. Stir in the blueberry yogurt.

Refrigerate the filling until almost set, about 1 hour. Mix in the fresh blueberries. Mound the filling into the crust.

Refrigerate the pie 2 to 3 hours or until firm. Cut into 8 slices.

Per Serving: Calories: 176; % Calories from fat: 31; Fat (gm): 5.8; Saturated fat (gm): 1.3; Cholesterol (mg): 2.7; Sodium (mg): 320; Protein (gm): 5.3; Carbohydrate (gm): 24.2
Exchanges: Milk: 0.0; Vegetable: 0.0; Fruit: 0.0; Bread: 1.5; Meat: 0.0; Fat: 1.0

This pie is quick and easy to assemble, especially if you purchase a crust and reduced-fat brownies.

CHOCOLATE YOGURT PIE

MAKES 8 SERVINGS, 1 SLICE PER SERVING

　　1　(9-inch) Graham Cracker Crust (recipe on Page 126)
　3 1/2　cups plain low-fat yogurt
　　1　packet (1/2 ounce) sugar-free hot cocoa mix
　　6　reduced-fat brownies, crumbled, store-bought or
　　　　homemade (recipe on Page 124)

Refrigerate the crust for at least 20 minutes.

Mix yogurt with cocoa mix in large bowl. Measure 2 cups of crumbled brownies and fold into the yogurt mixture. Mound the filling into the crust. Cover pie lightly with aluminum foil.

Freeze the pie for 2 hours or until firm.

Just before serving, remove the pie from the freezer and let stand at room temperature to soften slightly. Cut into 8 slices.

Per Serving: Calories: 221; % Calories from fat: 35; Fat (gm): 8.5; Saturated fat (gm): 2.5; Cholesterol (mg): 22.7; Sodium (mg): 343; Protein (gm): 8.8; Carbohydrate (gm): 26.8
Exchanges: Milk: 0.0; Vegetable: 0.0; Fruit: 0.0; Bread: 2.0; Meat: 0.0; Fat: 1.5

To test a cake for doneness, insert a cake tester or bamboo skewer into center of the cake. When it comes out clean and dry, the cake is done. Drizzle the cake with a small amount of Chocolate Sauce (see next recipe) if you can afford a few more calories.

FUDGE CAKE

MAKES 10 SERVINGS, 1 SLICE PER SERVING

Butter-flavored nonstick cooking spray
$1/4$ cup skim milk
$1/2$ cup cocoa powder
$1/4$ cup reduced-fat margarine
$1/2$ cup sugar
$1 1/2$ teaspoons vanilla
2 eggs
2 cups sifted cake flour
$3/4$ teaspoon each: baking soda and baking powder
$3/4$ cup low-fat buttermilk

Position oven rack in center of oven and preheat oven to 350 degrees F. Lightly coat a 9-inch springform pan with cooking spray. Line springform with aluminum foil and lightly spray again.

Scald milk in a small saucepan over medium heat. Whisk in cocoa powder. Cool.

Beat margarine with sugar in a large mixing bowl with electric mixer until light and creamy. Stir in cocoa mixture, vanilla, and eggs.

Sift flour with baking powder and baking soda in a separate bowl. Add the dry ingredients to egg mixture alternately with buttermilk. Pour batter into the springform pan.

Bake for 40 minutes or until toothpick or cake tester inserted in center comes out clean. Cool on wire rack. Remove springform sides and foil. Cut into 10 slices and serve.

Per Serving: Calories: 163; % Calories from fat: 17; Fat (gm): 3.2; Saturated fat (gm): 0.8; Cholesterol (mg): 0.9; Sodium (mg): 195; Protein (gm): 4.6; Carbohydrate (gm): 30.5
Exchanges: Milk: 0.0; Vegetable: 0.0; Fruit: 0.0; Bread: 2.0; Meat: 0.0; Fat: 0.5

For a thicker sauce, remove $1/2$ cup of the sauce and mix it with $1^1/2$ teaspoons cornstarch. Return the mixture to the pan and continue cooking, stirring often, until the sauce thickens slightly. If you want a richer sauce, substitute 1 cup of fat-free half-and-half for 1 cup of the water. The sauce is even better the next day.

◔ **LOW CARB**
☙ **LOW FAT**
◇ **LOW SODIUM**

CHOCOLATE SAUCE

MAKES 1½ CUPS SAUCE, OR 12 SERVINGS OF 2 TABLESPOONS

$1/2$ cup cocoa powder

$1^1/2$ cups water

$1/3$ cup sugar

$1^1/2$ teaspoons vanilla

Whisk the cocoa with $3/4$ cup of the cold water in a saucepan over medium heat. Add the remaining $3/4$ cup of water and the sugar. Bring the mixture to a boil. Reduce the heat to a simmer. Cook for 3 minutes stirring often.

Remove sauce from heat and cool. Stir in the vanilla.

Spoon the sauce into a container and refrigerate covered until ready to serve. Stir before serving.

Per Serving: Calories: 30; % Calories from fat: 11; Fat (gm): 0.5; Saturated fat (gm): 0.3; Cholesterol (mg): 0; Sodium (mg): 1; Protein (gm): 0.7; Carbohydrate (gm): 7.4
Exchanges: Milk: 0.0; Vegetable: 0.0; Fruit: 0.0; Bread: 0.5; Meat: 0.0; Fat: 0.0

Bread pudding is comfort food at its best. To measure sliced bread pieces, tear it into small pieces and pack it in a measuring cup.

🐮 LOW FAT

APPLE BREAD PUDDING

MAKES 6 SERVINGS, 1 SQUARE PER SERVING

2 cups tightly packed day-old multigrain bread pieces

1 quart skim milk or reduced fat (2%) milk

1 cup chopped, peeled apples, such as Granny Smith

$1/4$ cup egg substitute

2 lightly beaten egg whites

$1 1/2$ teaspoons vanilla

$1/4$ cup sugar

Position oven rack in center of oven and preheat oven to 350 degrees F. Layer bread in a 2-quart baking dish. Pour milk over the bread. Using a fork, push bread pieces down into the milk so the bread is covered. Let stand for 15 minutes, stirring mixture once or twice.

Stir apples into bread mixture. Mix together egg substitute, egg whites, vanilla, and sugar in mixing bowl. Pour egg mixture over bread and apples.

Set baking dish in a larger baking pan. Place the baking pan in the oven. Pour hot water halfway up sides of the baking pan. Bake for 1 hour and 15 minutes or until pudding is set and lightly browned. Cut into 6 squares and serve warm.

....

Per Serving: Calories: 132; % Calories from fat: 4; Fat (gm): 0.6; Saturated fat (gm): 0.2; Cholesterol (mg): 3.3; Sodium (mg): 142; Protein (gm): 8.9; Carbohydrate (gm): 23.6
Exchanges: Milk: 1.0; Vegetable: 0.0; Fruit: 0.5; Bread: 0.5; Meat: 0.0; Fat: 0.0

The development of no-sugar-added fruit spreads has been a boon for people watching their carbohydrate intake. Fruit spreads help enrich flavors while reducing the amount of sugar needed in a recipe.

☻ LOW FAT
◇ LOW SODIUM

APRICOT JELLY ROLL

MAKES 15 SERVINGS, 1 SLICE PER SERVING

Butter-flavored nonstick cooking spray

2 eggs

3 egg whites

$^1/_3$ cup sugar

1 teaspoon vanilla

$^3/_4$ cup all-purpose flour

2 tablespoons cornstarch

1 teaspoon baking powder

1 $^1/_4$ cups no-sugar-added apricot fruit spread

Preheat oven to 400 degrees F. Lightly coat a nonstick 10 x 15-inch jelly roll pan with cooking spray. Line the pan with parchment baking paper or waxed paper.

Beat the eggs and whites until light and foamy. Sprinkle the sugar over egg mixture and beat for 2 minutes. Stir in the vanilla.

Sift together the flour, cornstarch, and baking powder in a mixing bowl. Stir half of the flour mixture into the egg mixture. Once the first batch of flour is incorporated, stir in the remaining flour.

Spread the batter evenly in the jelly roll pan. Bake for 10 to 12 minutes or until the cake is golden and springs back to the touch.

Set a clean kitchen towel on the counter top and cover with aluminum foil. Loosen the edges of the cake with the tip of a knife. Flip the pan over and remove the cake. Gently peel the parchment off the cake.

Roll the cake up jelly-roll style, using the towel as a guide and to handle the roll. Leave the cake rolled in the towel until it cools completely.

Unroll the cake and coat it with apricot spread. Re-roll the cake removing the foil and the towel. Cut the roll into 15 (1-inch) slices.

Per Serving: Calories: 111; % Calories from fat: 6; Fat (gm): 0.7; Saturated fat (gm): 0.2; Cholesterol (mg): 28.3; Sodium (mg): 52; Protein (gm): 2.2; Carbohydrate (gm): 23.6
Exchanges: Milk: 0.0; Vegetable: 0.0; Fruit: 0.5; Bread: 1.0; Meat: 0.0; Fat: 0.0

A grunt is an old New England dessert recipe. The name comes from the sound the berries make while cooking. This easy dessert is cooked on top of the stove.

🐮 **LOW FAT**
◇ **LOW SODIUM**

BLUEBERRY GRUNT

MAKES 6 (¾-CUP) SERVINGS

> 5 cups fresh blueberries or raspberries
> ¼ cup sugar
> 1 ½ cups water
> 2 tablespoons cornstarch
> 2 tablespoons lemon juice
> Sugar-free, nondairy whipped topping, optional

Stir together 2 cups of the berries, sugar, water, cornstarch, and lemon juice in a saucepan. Cook over medium-low heat until mixture thickens and bubbles, about 3 minutes.

Spoon the fruit mixture into dessert cups and refrigerate, lightly covered, until cold.

Just before serving, scatter remaining berries on top of each cup. Serve with sugar-free whipped topping if desired.

TIP: Try a combination of berries for an interesting flavor and color.

Per Serving: Calories: 110; % Calories from fat: 3; Fat (gm): 0.5; Saturated fat (gm): 0; Cholesterol (mg): 0; Sodium (mg): 8; Protein (gm): 0.8; Carbohydrate (gm): 27.8
Exchanges: Milk: 0.0; Vegetable: 0.0; Fruit: 2.0; Bread: 0.0; Meat: 0.0; Fat: 0.0

Soft custard is not difficult to prepare. Serve the smooth, creamy custard with seasonal berries or other fruit.

☃ LOW FAT
◇ LOW SODIUM

OLD-FASHIONED SOFT CUSTARD

MAKES 6 (½-CUP) SERVINGS

   1 cup egg substitute
  ¼ cup sugar
   3 tablespoons all-purpose flour
2½ cups reduced-fat (2%) milk, scalded and cooled
1½ teaspoons vanilla

Whisk together the egg substitute, sugar, and flour in mixing bowl until light and frothy.

Pour mixture into a heavy saucepan over low heat or a double boiler over simmering water. Slowly whisk in milk. Continue simmering, stirring constantly, until the mixture thickens and coats a metal spoon, about 10 minutes. Remove the pan from heat and stir in the vanilla.

Cool the custard slightly and pour it into a bowl. Cover the custard with plastic wrap, making sure the wrap touches the surface of the custard to help prevent a skin from forming on top.

....

Per Serving: Calories: 119; % Calories from fat: 15; Fat (gm): 2; Saturated fat (gm): 1.2; Cholesterol (mg): 8.1; Sodium (mg): 128; Protein (gm): 7.8; Carbohydrate (gm): 16.7
Exchanges: Milk: 0.0; Vegetable: 0.0; Fruit: 0.0; Bread: 1.0; Meat: 1.0; Fat: 0.0

Because angel food cake does not freeze well, wrap individual slices tightly in plastic wrap and they will keep for up to 3 days. For special occasions, serve this cake with Fresh Peach Sauce (recipe on Page 141).

⏣ **LOW CARB**
🐄 **LOW FAT**
◇ **LOW SODIUM**

ANGEL FOOD CAKE

SERVES 12, 1 SLICE PER SERVING

1 1/2 cups egg whites, at room temperature (about 10 to 12 egg whites)

1 teaspoon cream of tartar

1/2 cup sugar

1 1/4 teaspoons vanilla

3/4 cup cake flour, sifted twice

Position oven rack in center of oven and preheat the oven to 350 degrees F. Cut a sheet of waxed paper to fit the bottom of a 10-inch nonstick tube cake pan with legs.

Beat the egg whites in a large bowl with electric mixer until light and foamy. Sprinkle in cream of tartar and sugar. Continue beating until egg whites are firm and hold peaks. Gently fold in vanilla with rubber spatula.

Sprinkle the flour, 1/3 at a time, over the egg white mixture. Using a rubber spatula, gently fold flour mixture into egg white mixture. Do not overmix or egg white mixture will deflate. Carefully spoon the batter into tube cake pan.

Bake for 50 to 55 minutes or until the cake is lightly browned on top and springs back when touched. Invert tube cake pan on its legs to cool. Loosen cake from the pan with a long knife run around the edges. Remove the cake from pan when cooled completely. Cut the cake into 12 slices with serrated bread knife.

TIP: If your tube cake pan does not have legs, invert the pan over a bottle with a tall, narrow neck.

Per Serving: Calories: 73; % Calories from fat: 1; Fat (gm): 0.1; Saturated fat (gm): 0; Cholesterol (mg): 0; Sodium (mg): 50; Protein (gm): 3.8; Carbohydrate (gm): 13.8
Exchanges: Milk: 0.0; Vegetable: 0.0; Fruit: 0.0; Bread: 1.0; Meat: 0.0; Fat: 0.0

Fresh fruit sauces are a wonderful way to add more fruit to your diet. Experiment with different soft fruits such as plums and nectarines, or a blend of fruits.

☙ LOW FAT
◇ LOW SODIUM

FRESH PEACH SAUCE

MAKES 6 SERVINGS

2 cups chopped, peeled fresh ripe peaches
2 tablespoons no-sugar-added orange or peach
    fruit spread
1/2 cup unsweetened orange juice

Mix together peaches, fruit spread, and orange juice in a saucepan. Cook over medium-high heat until mixture boils. Reduce heat and simmer, uncovered, until peaches are soft and sauce thickens slightly, 5 to 8 minutes. Stir occasionally.

Remove saucepan from heat and cool mixture in pan. Mash mixture with back of a fork.

Spoon the sauce into a covered container and refrigerate until ready to serve.

Per Serving: Calories: 72; % Calories from fat: 2; Fat (gm): 0.1; Saturated fat (gm): 0; Cholesterol (mg): 0; Sodium (mg): 0; Protein (gm): 0.9; Carbohydrate (gm): 18.2
Exchanges: Milk: 0.0; Vegetable: 0.0; Fruit: 1.0; Bread: 0.0; Meat: 0.0; Fat: 0.0

Serve chocolate cupcakes with a glass of cold milk. If you wish, sprinkle cupcakes with a light dusting of confectioner's sugar.

CHOCOLATE CUPCAKES

MAKES 12 CUPCAKES, 1 CUPCAKE PER SERVING

Butter-flavored nonstick cooking spray
1/4 cup skim milk
1/2 cup unsweetened cocoa powder
1/4 cup reduced-fat margarine
1/2 cup sugar
1 1/2 teaspoons vanilla extract
2 eggs
2 cups sifted cake flour
3/4 teaspoon baking soda
3/4 teaspoon baking powder
3/4 cup low-fat buttermilk
Confectioner's sugar for sprinkling, optional

Position rack in center of oven and preheat oven to 350 degrees F. Lightly coat a nonstick muffin pan with cooking spray.

In a small saucepan, scald milk over medium heat. Whisk in cocoa. Cool.

Using electric mixer, beat margarine with sugar. Stir in cocoa mixture, vanilla extract, and eggs. Sift flower with baking powder and baking soda. Add dry ingredients to egg mixture, alternating with buttermilk.

Pour batter into pan. Bake for about 20 minutes or until toothpick or cake tester inserted in center of a cupcake comes out clean and dry. Cool cupcakes in pan on wire rack. Turn out of pan.

Lightly sprinkle cupcakes with confectioner's sugar if desired.

Per Serving: Calories: 143; % Calories from fat: 21; Fat (gm): 3.5; Saturated fat (gm): 1; Cholesterol (mg): 36.1; Sodium (mg): 185; Protein (gm): 3.9; Carbohydrate (gm): 25.4
Exchanges: Milk: 0.0; Vegetable: 0.0; Fruit: 0.0; Bread: 1.5; Meat: 0.0; Fat: 1.0

Poached pears are so easy to make. Delicious on their own, they can be dressed up for company with no-sugar-added ice cream or Chocolate Sauce (recipe on Page 108).

☺ **LOW FAT**
◇ **LOW SODIUM**

EASY POACHED PEARS

MAKES 6 SERVINGS, 1 PEAR PER SERVING

6 ripe, firm pears, peeled but stem intact
6 cups water or more
1 tablespoon lime juice
1 teaspoon ground cinnamon or 2 cinnamon sticks

Place pears upright in a medium saucepan. Pour in enough water to cover pears. Add lime juice and cinnamon. Bring mixture to a boil over medium heat. Reduce heat to a simmer.

Cook for 10 minutes or until pears are tender when pierced with the tip of a sharp knife.

Remove pears with a slotted spoon to a serving plate or individual dessert bowls. Cool.

TIP: Substitute peaches for pears.

Per Serving: Calories: 100; % Calories from fat: 5; Fat (gm): 0.7; Saturated fat (gm): 0; Cholesterol (mg): 0; Sodium (mg): 0; Protein (gm): 0.7; Carbohydrate (gm): 25.6
Exchanges: Milk: 0.0; Vegetable: 0.0; Fruit: 1.5; Bread: 0.0; Meat: 0.0; Fat: 0.0

*For a more intense flavor, add 1 teaspoon anise flavoring
and 2 tablespoons grated lemon rind to the dough.*

🔥 **LOW CARB**
🐮 **LOW FAT**
◇ **LOW SODIUM**

BISCOTTI

MAKES 22 SLICES, 1 SLICE PER SERVING

> Butter-flavored nonstick cooking spray
> 2 cups all-purpose flour
> 1/3 cup sugar
> 2 tablespoons anise seeds or poppy seeds
> 1 teaspoon baking powder
> 1/2 teaspoon baking soda
> 1 cup egg substitute

Position a rack in the center of the oven and preheat oven to 325 degrees F. Lightly coat a nonstick baking sheet with cooking spray.

Combine flour, sugar, anise seeds, baking powder, baking soda, and egg substitute in a bowl using electric mixer.

Knead the dough with clean, damp hands until it holds together. Add a little more flour if necessary during kneading to keep the dough from sticking.

Shape the dough into a log almost the length of the baking sheet.

Lightly coat the top of the log with cooking spray.

Bake for 35 minutes or until log becomes firm to the touch. Remove from oven and cool slightly on baking sheet. While log is still warm, cut diagonally into scant 1/2-inch–thick slices.

Lay slices cut side down on baking sheet. Bake another 15 minutes or until biscotti are crisp. Cool completely on wire racks. Store in an airtight container in a cool, dry place.

Per Serving: Calories: 60; % Calories from fat: 3; Fat (gm): 0; Saturated fat (gm): 0; Cholesterol (mg): 0; Sodium (mg): 69; Protein (gm): 2.4; Carbohydrate (gm): 12.1
Exchanges: Milk: 0.0; Vegetable: 0.0; Fruit: 0.0; Bread: 1.0; Meat: 0.0; Fat: 0.0

For something different, bake the apples in sugar-free soda such as cherry, lemon, or lime instead of water. The dish can be served hot, warm, or cold.

⦿ LOW CARB
🐄 LOW FAT
◇ LOW SODIUM

BAKED APPLES

MAKES 8 SERVINGS, ½ APPLE PER SERVING

4 large apples, cored
2 teaspoons raisins
2 tablespoons chopped walnuts
2 teaspoons sugar
½ cup water

Position rack in center of oven and preheat oven to 400 degrees F. Peel away skin from top ¼ of each apple. Arrange apples in a pie plate.

Combine raisins, walnuts, and sugar in a small bowl. Stuff each apple with mixture.

Add water to the pie plate. Bake for 25 minutes or until apples are tender.

Slice apples in half and serve in individual dishes. Spoon any sauce over the apples.

Per Serving: Calories: 66; % Calories from fat: 19; Fat (gm): 1.5; Saturated fat (gm): 0.2; Cholesterol (mg): 0; Sodium (mg): 0; Protein (gm): 0.5; Carbohydrate (gm): 14.1
Exchanges: Milk: 0.0; Vegetable: 0.0; Fruit: 1.0; Bread: 0.0; Meat: 0.0; Fat: 0.0

Couscous is a tiny pasta used in Middle Eastern salads, side dishes, and desserts. Whole-wheat couscous is available at natural foods stores. Most supermarkets stock conventional couscous made from white flour. Cook extra couscous or brown rice for dinner to have enough left to make dessert the next day.

☻ LOW FAT
◇ LOW SODIUM

SWEET COUSCOUS

MAKES 6 (½-CUP) SERVINGS

1 cup cooked couscous, preferably whole-wheat, prepared according to package directions using water or skim milk, omitting salt

¼ cup golden raisins

3 tablespoons toasted pine nuts (see Tip)

2 tablespoons warm honey

Toss warm couscous with raisins and pine nuts in a mixing bowl.

Spoon mixture into individual dessert dishes and drizzle with warm honey.

TIP: To toast pine nuts, heat a small, dry skillet over medium-high heat. Add pine nuts and cook, stirring constantly, until fragrant and starting to brown. Take care not to burn.

Add a sprinkle of ground cinnamon for extra flavor.

Per Serving: Calories: 182; % Calories from fat: 12; Fat (gm): 2.4; Saturated fat (gm): 0.4; Cholesterol (mg): 0; Sodium (mg): 4; Protein (gm): 5.2; Carbohydrate (gm): 35.6
Exchanges: Milk: 0.0; Vegetable: 0.0; Fruit: 0.0; Bread: 0.0; Meat: 0.0; Fat: 0.0

Meringues bake better on a dry day. For optimum volume, use fresh eggs that have stood on the counter until they are at room temperature. To quickly warm eggs, place them in a bowl of tepid water.

⏣ **LOW CARB**
🐄 **LOW FAT**
◇ **LOW SODIUM**

ORANGE MERINGUE COOKIES

MAKES ABOUT 18 COOKIES, 1 COOKIE PER SERVING

Nonstick cooking spray
2 egg whites, at room temperature
⅓ cup sugar
1 teaspoon cream of tartar
1 teaspoon orange extract

Preheat oven to 275 degrees F. Lightly coat a baking sheet with cooking spray. Line the sprayed sheet with aluminum foil or parchment baking paper.

Beat the egg whites with an electric mixer until soft peaks form. Sprinkle the egg whites with the sugar and cream of tartar. Continue beating until hard peaks form. Add the orange extract and fold in gently by hand with a rubber spatula.

Drop the batter by the tablespoonful onto the baking sheet.

Bake 45 minutes. Turn the oven off and cool the cookies in the oven with the oven door closed. The cookies should be firm to the touch. Store the cookies in an airtight container.

Per Serving: Calories: 17; % Calories from fat: 0; Fat (gm): 0; Saturated fat (gm): 0; Cholesterol (mg): 0; Sodium (mg): 6; Protein (gm): 0.4; Carbohydrate (gm): 3.7
Exchanges: Milk: 0.0; Vegetable: 0.0; Fruit: 0.0; Bread: 0.25; Meat: 0.0; Fat: 0.0

This special dessert should be enjoyed only occasionally because it is still relatively high in carbohydrates, although greatly improved from a health standpoint over a conventional banana split.

🐮 LOW FAT
◇ LOW SODIUM

BANANA SPLITS

MAKES 4 SERVINGS, ½ BANANA PER SERVING

Butter-flavored nonstick cooking spray

2 firm ripe bananas, peeled and split lengthwise

2 cups no-sugar-added, nonfat vanilla ice cream

8 tablespoons Chocolate Sauce, (see recipe Page 108)

Divide bananas among 4 banana split boats. (If you do not have banana split boats, slice the bananas into dessert bowls.) Scoop ice cream over the bananas. Drizzle each banana split with 2 tablespoons Chocolate Sauce.

VARIATION: To make Bananas Foster, lightly coat a frying pan with butter-flavored nonstick cooking spray. Cook peeled, split bananas until warm and starting to brown. Place bananas on serving dish and top with no-sugar-added frozen vanilla yogurt. Drizzle with a tablespoon of sugar-free caramel sauce.

SERVING SUGGESTION: Add a few tablespoons of sugar-free nondairy whipped topping if you like. For a simple strawberry sauce, crush fresh strawberries with a packet of sugar substitute.

Per Serving: Calories: 174; % Calories from fat: 4; Fat (gm): 0.8; Saturated fat (gm): 0.4; Cholesterol (mg): 0; Sodium (mg): 51; Protein (gm): 4.3; Carbohydrate (gm): 40.2
Exchanges: Milk: 0.0; Vegetable: 0.0; Fruit: 1.0; Bread: 1.5; Meat: 0.0; Fat: 0.0

For extra flavor, add dash of salt, $1/4$ cup golden raisins, and $1/2$ teaspoon of ground cinnamon.

☻ **LOW FAT**
◇ **LOW SODIUM**

CUSTARD RICE PUDDING

MAKES 6 SERVINGS

Butter-flavored nonstick cooking spray
2 cups cooked white, or brown, rice, cooled
1 quart skim, or reduced-fat (2%), milk
$3/4$ cup egg substitute
$1/4$ cup sugar
$1 1/2$ teaspoons vanilla

Lightly coat a $1 1/2$-quart baking dish with cooking spray. Set a pan large enough to hold the baking dish in the oven and fill it halfway with warm water. Preheat the oven to 350 degrees F.

Combine the rice with the milk, egg substitute, sugar, and vanilla in the baking dish. Break up any clumps of rice.

Set the baking dish in the water-filled pan. Bake for 1 hour and 15 minutes or until the custard is set and lightly browned around the edges.

Per Serving: Calories: 197; % Calories from fat: 14; Fat (gm): 2.9; Saturated fat (gm): 1; Cholesterol (mg): 109.5; Sodium (mg): 117; Protein (gm): 10.1; Carbohydrate (gm): 31.2
Exchanges: Milk: 1.0; Vegetable: 0.0; Fruit: 0.0; Bread: 1.5; Meat: 0.0; Fat: 0.0

Light brown sugar should not be confused with brown sugar substitute. Brown sugar comes in dark and light colors that have nothing to do with the carbohydrate and calorie counts, which are the same as regular sugar.

◇ **LOW SODIUM**

CARAMELIZED APPLE SLICES

MAKES 6 SERVINGS

Butter-flavored nonstick cooking spray
3 tablespoons reduced-fat margarine
4 cups sliced, peeled and cored apples
$1/4$ cup light brown sugar
$1/4$ teaspoon ground cinnamon

Lightly coat a nonstick frying pan with cooking spray. Melt the margarine over medium heat. Add the apples and sugar. Fry apples until golden and caramelized. Sprinkle with cinnamon.

Spoon apples into dessert dishes and serve warm.

Per Serving: Calories: 103; % Calories from fat: 25; Fat (gm): 3.1; Saturated fat (gm): 0.5; Cholesterol (mg): 0; Sodium (mg): 71; Protein (gm): 0.1; Carbohydrate (gm): 20.2
Exchanges: Milk: 0.0; Vegetable: 0.0; Fruit: 1.5; Bread: 0.0; Meat: 0.0; Fat: 0.5

Children will enjoy threading fruit cubes on their own skewers. Vary the fruit according to family preferences and seasonal availability.

🐄 **LOW FAT**
◇ **LOW SODIUM**

GRILLED FRUIT KABOBS

MAKES 6 SERVINGS, 1 KABOB PER SERVING

    Butter-flavored nonstick cooking spray
1 cup cubed pineapple
1 cup thickly sliced peaches
1 cup banana chunks
6 (8-inch) wooden skewers

Lightly coat the indoor electric grill or stovetop grill with cooking spray. Heat according to manufacturer's directions.

Thread the fruit on the skewers. Grill the kabobs a few minutes, turning on all sides, until warm and grill marks show.

Per Serving: Calories: 60; % Calories from fat: 4; Fat (gm): 0.3; Saturated fat (gm): 0.1; Cholesterol (mg): 0; Sodium (mg): 1; Protein (gm): 0.8; Carbohydrate (gm): 15.4
Exchanges: Milk: 0.0; Vegetable: 0.0; Fruit: 1.0; Bread: 0.0; Meat: 0.0; Fat: 0.0

With store-bought angel food cake, this dessert is a breeze to make as well as lower in fat and calories than the traditional dessert.

🐮 **LOW FAT**
◇ **LOW SODIUM**

STRAWBERRY SHORTCAKE

MAKES 4 SERVINGS, 1 SLICE PER SERVING

- 4 slices angel food cake, store-bought or homemade (recipe on Page 139)
- 1 cup sugar-free nondairy whipped topping
- 3 cups sliced strawberries
- 2 tablespoons sugar or sugar substitute

Arrange a slice of angel food cake on each plate. Spoon whipped topping on cake and sprinkle with strawberries and sugar.

Per Serving: Calories: 168; % Calories from fat: 13; Fat (gm): 2.5; Saturated fat (gm): 1; Cholesterol (mg): 0; Sodium (mg): 61; Protein (gm): 4.4; Carbohydrate (gm): 31.4
Exchanges: Milk: 0.0; Vegetable: 0.0; Fruit: 1.0; Bread: 1.0; Meat: 0.0; Fat: 0.5

*Freeze the strawberries in a single layer on a baking sheet.
Pack the frozen berries in a large, resealable plastic food
storage bag. If you like your slushie sweeter, add 1 or 2
packets of sugar substitute to the purée.*

♨ **LOW CARB**
🐮 **LOW FAT**
◇ **LOW SODIUM**

STRAWBERRY SLUSHIE

MAKES 8 (1-CUP) SERVINGS

   2 pints fresh strawberries, hulled and frozen
1/2 cup no-sugar-added orange juice

Purée the berries with the orange juice in a food processor or
blender. Spoon the mixture into glasses and serve.

....

Per Serving: Calories: 41; % Calories from fat: 9; Fat (gm): 0.5; Saturated fat (gm): 0;
Cholesterol (mg): 0; Sodium (mg): 1; Protein (gm): 0.8; Carbohydrate (gm): 9.6
Exchanges: Milk: 0.0; Vegetable: 0.0; Fruit: 0.5; Bread: 0.0; Meat: 0.0; Fat: 0.0

Bananas contain fiber, potassium, and other healthful nutrients that make them a good food choice, although in moderation because of their relatively high carbohydrate content. Puréed bananas create a smooth, creamy consistency, almost like ice cream.

🐮 LOW FAT
◇ LOW SODIUM

BANANA CHOCOLATE SHERBET

MAKES 6 SERVINGS

5 ripe bananas, peeled and cut into chunks
2 tablespoons cocoa powder
1 packet sugar substitute

Purée the bananas with the cocoa powder and sugar substitute in a food processor or blender. Spoon the mixture into a covered container and freeze for 2 hours or until firm.

When ready to serve, scoop the sherbet into footed glasses. Serve immediately.

Per Serving: Calories: 95; % Calories from fat: 6; Fat (gm): 0.7; Saturated fat (gm): 0.3; Cholesterol (mg): 0; Sodium (mg): 1; Protein (gm): 1.3; Carbohydrate (gm): 24.2
Exchanges: Milk: 0.0; Vegetable: 0.0; Fruit: 1.5; Bread: 0.0; Meat: 0.0; Fat: 0.0

To vary the flavor of the sherbet, substitute mango or peaches for the pears, or try a mixture of fruits. Use very ripe fruit for the best flavor. If you wish, forego the cones and serve the sherbet in a dish.

🐮 LOW FAT
◇ LOW SODIUM

PEAR SHERBET IN A CONE

MAKES 6 SERVINGS, ½ CUP SHERBET AND 1 CONE PER SERVING

4 large ripe pears, peeled, cored, and sliced
½ to ¾ cup evaporated skimmed milk (not condensed)
2 tablespoons sugar
2 tablespoons lemon juice
¾ teaspoon vanilla
6 small ice cream cones

Blend the pears with the milk, sugar, lemon juice, and vanilla in a blender. Spoon the mixture into a shallow pan and cover with plastic wrap. Freeze until firm, about 2 hours.

When ready to serve, let pan stand at room temperature for 5 to 10 minutes to soften slightly. Scoop or scrape the sherbet into the cones.

Per Serving: Calories: 117; % Calories from fat: 5; Fat (gm): 0.8; Saturated fat (gm): 0.1; Cholesterol (mg): 0.9; Sodium (mg): 30; Protein (gm): 2.4; Carbohydrate (gm): 26.8
Exchanges: Milk: 0.0; Vegetable: 0.0; Fruit: 0.0; Bread: 1.5; Meat: 0.0; Fat: 0.0

A classic summer treat gets a no-sugar makeover. For a frosty effect, serve the float in a mug or heavy-bottomed glass that has been chilled in the freezer.

○ **LOW CARB**
♨ **LOW FAT**
◇ **LOW SODIUM**

ROOT BEER FLOAT

MAKES 1 SERVING

1 can (8 ounces) sugar-free root beer
$^1/_2$ cup no-sugar-added vanilla ice cream

Pour root beer into a tall glass. Add ice cream scoop. Serve immediately.

Per Serving: Calories: 90; % Calories from fat: 30; Fat (gm): 3; Saturated fat (gm): 1.5; Cholesterol (mg): 10; Sodium (mg): 95; Protein (gm): 3; Carbohydrate (gm): 13
Exchanges: Milk: 0.0; Vegetable: 0.0; Fruit: 0.0; Bread: 1.0; Meat: 0.0; Fat: 0.5

INDEX